HUGH LA

Anglican classics in the Fyfield series

Lancelot Andrewes
Selected Writings

Richard Hooker
Ecclesiastical Polity: Selections

William Law
Selected Writings

Jeremy Taylor
Selected Writings

HUGH LATIMER

Sermons

Edited with an introduction by
ARTHUR POLLARD

FyfieldBooks

Published in Great Britain in 2000 by
Carcanet Press Limited
4th Floor, Conavon Court
12–16 Blackfriars Street
Manchester M3 5BQ

A CIP catalogue record for this book
is available from the British Library.

ISBN 1 85754 458 7

The publisher acknowledges financial assistance
from the Arts Council of England.

Set in 10/12pt Palatino by XL Publishing Services, Tiverton
Printed and bound in England by SRP Ltd, Exeter

Contents

Introduction

'Be of good cheer, master Ridley, and play the man. We shall this day light such a candle, by God's grace, in England, as I trust shall never be put out.' These words, spoken by Hugh Latimer as he and Ridley were about to be martyred at the stake, more than any others encapsulate the spirit of the Protestant Reformation of the sixteenth century. Besides that, they also illustrate Latimer's own sturdy courage and his capacity for ordinary but vivid and memorable imagery.

Latimer was born some time between 1490 and 1495 near Thurcaston (Leicestershire), the son of a yeoman farmer. Around 1506 he began his university education at Cambridge, becoming a Fellow of Clare Hall in 1510 and proceeding to an MA in 1514 and BD in 1524. It was a time of religious ferment. Just a few years before, in 1517, Luther had posted his famous 95 Theses on the church door at Wittenburg and the Reformation had begun. It was only the year before that the leading European humanist, Erasmus, had published his Greek New Testament. It was neither of these, however, who was to prove the decisive influence on Latimer, but one who was found among the earliest English Protestant martyrs. It is worth quoting Latimer himself:

Master Bilney, or rather Saint Bilney that suffered death for God's word sake; the same Bilney was the instrument whereby God called me to knowledge; for I may thank him, next to God, for that knowledge that I have in the word of God. For I was as obstinate a papist as any was in England, inasmuch that when I should be made bachelor of divinity, my whole oration went against Philip Melanchthon and against his opinions. Bilney heard me at that time, and perceived that I was zealous without knowledge: and he came to me afterward in my study, and desired me, for God's sake, to hear his confession. I did so; and, to say the truth, I learned more than before in many years. So from that time forward I began to smell the word of God, and forsook the school-doctors and such fooleries.

(First Sermon before the Duchess of Suffolk, Works, Parker Society, 1844, p. 334)

Latimer never did things by halves and his new-found faith soon aroused suspicions. On one occasion West, the Bishop of Ely, swept into church as Latimer was preaching. Latimer stopped to allow the episcopal party to take their places and then changed his subject completely and spoke of the office of a bishop! West thanked Latimer (how sincerely it is not difficult to guess) and then asked him to preach against Luther, to which Latimer replied by asking the bishop how he might be expected to refute the writings of someone he was not even permitted to read. West departed angry and with dark threats against the man who had proved too clever for him. Three years later, in 1528, Latimer had a brush with Wolsey, but two years after that Wolsey was no more.

Wolsey fell by reason of his failure to forward Henry VIII's divorce from Catherine of Aragon, whereas Latimer was active in securing support in Cambridge for the King. He preached before Henry for the first time in 1530, at the beginning of what was to prove a turbulent decade in England's political and religious history. Henry himself seems to have retained serious reservations about departure from the old faith, provided only that his own position was secure as head of the English church. Latimer found himself in trouble with the old guard in 1532 when he was examined by Convocation at the behest of Stokesley, the Bishop of London, and was made to confess to having preached erroneous doctrines. Then the pendulum swung the other way and he became Bishop of Worcester in 1535 – probably through the influence of Anne Boleyn, to whom he gave a bond for £200 six days after his consecration. In these years Latimer demonstrated that, whatever else he might be, he would not be an unpreaching prelate. Such indeed were to feel the lash of his tongue in his sermon before Convocation in 1536, in which he also condemned Romish ceremonies, icons and doctrines. It is also on record that, as he was to do later, he was forthright at this time in his assault on clerical luxury and neglect to care for the poor:

> On Sunday last, the Bishop of Worcester preached at Paul's Cross, and he said that bishops, abbots, priors, parsons, canons, resident priests and all were strong thieves; yea, dukes, lords and all… Bishops, abbots, with such others, should not have so many servants, nor so many dishes, but to go to their first foundation and keep hospitality to feed the needy people – not jolly fellows, with golden chains and velvet gowns.
>
> *(State Papers: Letters and Papers… of the Reign of Henry VIII*, X.462)

Plain spoken and vigorous, that is very Latimer.

It was at this time also (1536) that Latimer had some part in the composition of the Ten Articles, with their Protestant slant in accepting the need for spiritual sincerity on the part of the recipient of the sacrament and in the definition of justification as proceeding only from the free grace of God through the merits of Christ's death and passion. By 1539, however, reaction set in with the Catholic 'Six Articles', upon which Latimer resigned his see. He was forbidden to preach and lived in obscurity for some years. In 1546 he was arrested and imprisoned in the Tower of London, but then Henry died.

The young Edward VI succeeded under the protection first of Somerset, then of Northumberland. Latimer's hour had come, and from the next two years (1547–9) we have the series of sermons preached before the king. After 1550 he moved into semi-retirement, mainly at Grimsthorpe (Lincolnshire) in the household of the Duchess of Suffolk. He preached there also, but to a very different kind of audience, the village folk who lived and worked on the Duchess's estate.

Then the young king died; his sister Mary succeeded, and the Catholic reaction advanced in full sail. Latimer was sent to the Tower on 13 September 1553 and confined with his prospective fellow-martyrs, Cranmer and Ridley, until March of the following year, when they were transferred to the notorious Bocardo prison at Oxford's north gate. There followed all the mockery of pomp and circumstance with the university dignitaries, arrayed in all their finery, processing from place to place with their prisoners in tow. On Saturday, 14 April, there was a mass of the Holy Ghost at St Mary's, after which Cranmer first, then Ridley and finally Latimer were presented with a set of articles requiring them to subscribe to the idea of transubstantiation of the elements. All three refused and were taken away to different places of custody to prevent their conferring and to be returned separately the following week for more detailed cross-examination. Latimer's interrogators reminded him of the time that he had himself held and preached Romish doctrines, which the old man acknowledged to his sorrow and then with brave courage declared that he prayed daily for the queen that she might forsake her beliefs, and 'turn from this religion'.

The prisoners were condemned as heretics, but judicial sanction was required before sentence could be passed. A new commission therefore sat on 30 September. They were bidden to submit and recant. They refused and their fate was sealed on the next day. A fortnight later Latimer and Ridley were formally degraded. (Cranmer as archbishop had the right to appeal to the Pope – a further mockery in that he would have to go to Rome to do so and he was shut up in the Bocardo. His own execution was therefore delayed until March of the following year.) The next day, 16 October, the other two were led through the streets of Oxford, chained to the stake in the town ditch opposite Balliol and made to listen to a sermon by Dr Smith, himself a double-renegade. The fire was lit. No more needs to be said of this, one of the blackest days in English history. Latimer's punning image turned out true, for the candle that was lit that day has never been put out.

Latimer was above all else a preacher. For him instruction and therefore preaching, not the mass, was the ladder to heaven:

'God's instrument of salvation is preaching' (p. 58). The forty or so of his sermons which have been preserved, none of them precisely verbatim, must be merely a minute fraction of his total output. Nor were they the brief affairs of modern times; at the beginning of the last, which he preached before Edward VI, only half of which is reproduced here, he declared his intention to speak for three or four hours. What the teenage king made of that we can only imagine. These sermons in Lent 1550 represent Latimer at this most mature, but in their basic ideas and attitudes they are not essentially different from what he had thought and said in such earlier pieces as those on the Card and the Plough and what he had told his fellow-clerics in Convocation in 1536.

There is, of course, development, especially in doctrine. Thus in the Card sermons there are statements on human depravity and the uselessness of good works, views central to Reformed theology, but at this time there is still acceptance of the sacraments as *the* channels of grace. Twenty years later, in the Good Friday sermon before the king, that impassioned account of Christ's suffering, he can declare: 'What an horrible thing is sin, that no other thing would remedy and pay the ransom for it, but only the blood of our Saviour Christ' (p. 00). Doctrinal theology, however, was not Latimer's main interest, but rather what it meant practically in the life of the believer – and what could affect this other than the preacher? In his attacks on clerical abuse he was relentlessly consistent. In the Convocation sermon (1536) he told his fellow-clergy what he thought about them and their Romish practices (pp. 23–4), and he would repeat his charges in the sermon on the Plough twelve years later. Not surprisingly his main concern was their preaching or lack of it. He confronts them as an *Athanasius contra mundum*, himself alone against them all: 'You preach very seldom; and when ye do preach, do nothing but cumber them that preach truly... I would that Christian people should hear my doctrine... all your care is, that no lay man do read it' (First sermon to Convocation, *Works*, 1844, p. 38). As he put it in the Plough sermon, these were the 'strawberry' preachers, 'ministering it but once a year' (p. 35).

It was not just clerical abuses that Latimer exposed. In a time of considerable economic and social upheaval he found much that deserved his critical tongue. In the sermons before Edward VI, besides dwelling on the kingly office and the royal supremacy, he condemned corrupt magistrates, bribe-takers and, as befitted the son of a yeoman farmer, enclosers who transformed the rural economy so that whereas before there had been 'a great many of householders and inhabitants, there is now but a shepherd and his dog'. Besides the dispossession that this indicates, there was also extortion practised on the poor by one group after another:

> The physician, if the poor man be diseased, he can have no help without too much. And of the lawyer, the poor man can get no counsel expedition, nor help in his matter, except he give him too much. At merchants' hands no kind of ware can be had, except we give for it too much. You landlords, you rent-raisers... you have for your possessions yearly too much.
>
> (First Sermon before Edward VI, *Works*, pp. 98–9)

It was again the countryman who after the 1549 Rebellion spoke in the plainest egalitarian terms:

> They in Christ are equal with you... The poorest ploughman is in Christ equal with the greatest prince that is. Let them therefore have sufficient to maintain them... A plough-land must have sheep; yea, they must have sheep to dung their ground for bearing of corn... They must have other cattle: as horses to draw their plough... And kine for their milk and cheese, which they must live upon and pay their rents... Therefore, for God's love, restore their sufficient unto them, and search no more for what is the cause of rebellion.
>
> (Last Sermon before Edward VI, *Works*, p. 249)

I have quoted that passage also to illustrate Latimer's style: plain, direct, vivid, homely, forthright. It is there in his choice of the plough as the controlling image for his sermon; it is there again in the condemnation that he derives from a simple ordinary fruit when he speaks of strawberry preachers. It is present once more in the ingenious sarcasm that labels Judas as a cardinal and thereby casts the whole conclave as betrayers of Jesus and His religion. It appears in numerous examples that he draws from his own experience, whether it be the tale of the insomniac woman who went to St Thomas of Acres church where she claimed that she never failed to get a good nap (Sixth Sermon before Edward VI, *Works*, p. 201) or his illustration of the act of choosing by telling what had influenced him in deciding which Thames waterman to hire for his trip from Lambeth that day (ibid., p. 205). Latimer also cunningly employed diversions such as these to hold up his main discourse and to keep his hearers in suspense as to the process and progress of his argument. The obverse of this, however, was his tendency to garrulousness. His was the tongue of a ready speaker, and sometimes it is clear that he did not know when to stop. That said, Latimer, not surprisingly, was amongst the most popular preachers of his day. He never failed to speak his mind and nobody could forget what he had said.

The text in this collection is that of the Parker Society edition of Latimer's *Works*, ed G.E. Corrie, 1844, with a few minor alterations.

The First Sermon on the Card (1529)

Tu quis es? Which words are as much to say in English, 'Who art thou?' These be the words of the Pharisees, which were sent by the Jews unto St John Baptist in the wilderness, to have knowledge of him who he was: which words they spake unto him of an evil intent, thinking that he would have taken on him to be Christ, and so they would have had him done with their good wills, because they knew that he was more carnal, and given to their laws, than Christ indeed should be, as they perceived by their old prophecies; and also, because they marvelled much of his great doctrine, preaching, and baptizing, they were in doubt whether he was Christ or not: wherefore they said unto him, 'Who art thou?' Then answered St John, and confessed that he was not Christ.

Now here is to be noted the great and prudent answer of St John Baptist unto the Pharisees, that when they required of him who he was, he would not directly answer of himself what he was himself, but he said he was not Christ: by the which saying he thought to put the Jews and Pharisees out of their false opinion and belief towards him, in that they would have had him to exercise the office of Christ; and so declared further unto them of Christ, saying, 'He is in the midst of you and amongst you, whom ye know not, whose latchet of his shoe I am not worthy to unloose, or undo.' By this you may perceive that St John spake much in the laud and praise of Christ his Master, professing himself to be in no wise like unto him. So likewise it shall be necessary unto all men and women of this world, not to ascribe unto themselves any goodness of themselves, but all unto our Lord God, as shall appear hereafter, when this question aforesaid, 'Who art thou?' shall be moved unto them: not as the Pharisees did unto St John, of an evil purpose, but of a good and simple mind, as may appear hereafter.

Now then, according to the preacher's mind, let every man and woman, of a good and simple mind, contrary to the Pharisees' intent, ask this question, 'Who art thou?' This question must be moved to themselves, what they be of themselves, on this fashion: 'What art thou of thy only and natural generation between father and mother, when thou came into this world? What substance, what virtue, what goodness art thou of, by thyself?' Which question if thou rehearse oftentimes unto thyself, thou shalt well perceive and understand how thou shalt make answer unto it; which must be made on this wise: I am of myself, and by myself, coming from my natural father and mother, the child of the ire and indignation of God, the true inheritor of hell, a lump of sin, and working nothing of myself but all towards hell, except I have better help of another than I have of myself. Now we may see in what state we enter into this world, that we be of ourselves the true and just inheritors of hell, the children of the ire and indignation of Christ, working all towards hell, whereby we deserve of ourselves perpetual damnation, by the right judgment of God, and the true claim of ourselves; which unthrifty state that we be born unto is come unto us for our own deserts, as proveth well this example following.

Let it be admitted for the probation of this, that it might please the king's grace now being to accept into his favour a mean man, of a simple degree and birth, not born to any possession; whom the king's grace favoureth, not because this person hath of himself deserved any such favour, but that the king casteth this favour unto him of his own mere motion and fantasy: and for because the king's grace will more declare his favour unto him, he giveth unto this said man a thousand pounds in lands, to him and his heirs, on this condition, that he shall take upon himself to be the chief captain and defender of his town of Calais,[1] and to be true and faithful to him in the custody of the same, against the Frenchmen especially, above all other enemies.

1 Calais was in the possession of the English from the year 1346 until 1558, and the command of the garrison there was considered a trust of much importance.

This man taketh on him this charge, promising his fidelity thereunto. It chanceth in process of time, that by the singular acquaintance and frequent familiarity of this captain with the Frenchmen, these Frenchmen give unto the said captain of Calais a great sum of money, so that he will but be content and agreeable that they may enter into the said town of Calais by force of arms; and so thereby possess the same unto the crown of France. Upon this agreement the Frenchmen do invade the said town of Calais, alonely by the negligence of this captain.

Now the king's grace, hearing of this invasion, cometh with a great puissance to defend this his said town, and so by good policy of war overcometh the said Frenchmen, and entereth again into his said town of Calais. Then he, being desirous to know how these enemies of his came thither, maketh profound search and inquiry by whom this treason was conspired. By this search it was known and found his own captain to be the very author and the beginner of the betraying of it. The king, seeing the great infidelity of this person, dischargeth this man of his office, and taketh from him and from his heirs this thousand pounds of possessions. Think you not that the king doth use justice unto him, and all his posterity and heirs? Yes, truly: the said captain cannot deny himself but that he had true justice, considering how unfaithfully he behaved him to his prince, contrary to his own fidelity and promise. So likewise it was of our first father Adam. He had given unto him the spirit of science and knowledge, to work all goodness therewith: this said spirit was not given alonely unto him, but unto all his heirs and posterity. He has also delivered him the town of Calais, that is to say, paradise in earth, the most strong and fairest town in the world, to be in his custody. He nevertheless, by the instigation of these Frenchmen, that is to say, the temptation of the fiend, did obey unto their desire; and so he brake his promise and fidelity, the commandment of the everlasting King his master, in eating of the apple by him inhibited.

Now then the King, seeing this great treason in his captain, deposed him of the thousand pounds of possessions, that is to say, from everlasting life in glory, and all his heirs and posterity: for likewise as he had the spirit of science and knowledge, for him and his heirs; so in like manner, when he lost the same, his heirs also lost it by him and in him. So now this example proveth, that by our father Adam we had once in him the very inheritance of everlasting joy; and by him, and in him, again we lost the same.

The heirs of the captain of Calais could not by any manner of claim ask of the king the right and title of their father in the thousand pounds of possessions, by reason the king might answer and say unto them, that although their father deserved not of himself to enjoy so great possessions, yet he deserved by himself to lose them, and greater, committing so high treason, as he did, against his prince's commandments; whereby he had no wrong to lose his title, but was unworthy to have the same, and had therein true justice. Let not you think, which be his heirs, that if he had justice to lose his possessions, you have wrong to lose the same. In the same manner it may be answered unto all men and women now being, that if our father Adam had true justice to be excluded from his possession of everlasting glory in paradise, let us not think the contrary that be his heirs, but that we have no wrong in losing also the same; yea, we have true justice and right. Then in what miserable estate we be, that of the right and just title of our own deserts have lost the everlasting joy, and claim of ourselves to be true inheritors of hell! For he that committeth deadly sin willingly, bindeth himself to be inheritor of everlasting pain: and so did our forefather Adam willingly eat of the apple forbidden. Wherefore he was cast out of the everlasting joy in paradise into this corrupt world, amongst all vileness, whereby of himself he was not worthy to do any thing laudable or pleasant to God, evermore bound to corrupt affections and beastly appetites, transformed into the most uncleanest and variablest nature that was made under heaven; of whose seed and disposition all the world is lineally descended, insomuch that this evil nature is so fused and shed from one into another, that at this day there is no man nor woman living, that can of themselves wash away this abominable vileness: and so we must needs grant of ourselves to be in like displeasure unto God, as our forefather Adam was. By reason hereof, as I said, we be of ourselves the very children of the indignation and vengeance of God, the true inheritors of hell, and working all towards hell: which is the answer to this question, made to every man and woman, by themselves, 'Who art thou?'

And now, the world standing in this damnable state, cometh in the occasion of the incarnation of Christ. The Father in heaven, perceiving the frail nature of man, that he, by himself and of himself, could no nothing for himself, by his prudent wisdom sent down the second person in Trinity, his Son Jesus Christ, to declare unto man his pleasure and commandment: and so, at the Father's will, Christ took on him human nature, being willing to deliver man out of this miserable way, and was content to suffer cruel passion in shedding his blood for all mankind; and so left behind for our safeguard laws and ordinances, to keep us always in the right path unto everlasting life, as the evangelists, the sacraments, the commandments and so forth: which if we do keep and observe according to our profession, we shall answer better unto this question, 'Who art thou?' than we did before. For before thou didst enter into the sacrament of baptism, thou wert but a natural man, a natural woman; as I might say, a man, a woman: but after thou takest on thee Christ's religion, thou hast a longer name; for then thou art a christian man, a christian woman. Now then, seeing thou art a christian man, what shall be thy answer of this question, 'Who art thou?'

The answer of this question is, when I ask it unto myself, I must say that I am a christian man, a christian woman, the child of everlasting joy, through the merits of the bitter passion of Christ. This is a joyful answer. Here we may see how much we be bound and in danger unto God, that hath revived us from death to life, and saved us that were damned: which great benefit we cannot well consider; unless we do remember what we were of ourselves before we meddled with him or his laws; and the more we know our feeble nature, and set less by it, the more we shall conceive and know in our hearts what God hath done for us; and the more we know what God hath done for us, the less we shall set by ourselves, and the more we shall love and please God: so that in no condition we shall either know

5

ourselves or God, except we do utterly confess ourselves to be mere vileness and corruption. Well, now it is come unto this point, that we be christian men, christian women, I pray you what doth Christ require of a christian man, or of a christian woman? Christ requireth nothing else of a christian man or woman, but that they will observe his rule: for likewise as he is a good Augustine friar that keepeth well St Augustine's rule, so is he a good christian man that keepeth well Christ's rule.

Now then, what is Christ's rule? Christ's rule consisteth in many things, as in the commandments, and the works of mercy, and so forth. And for because I cannot declare Christ's rule unto you at one time, as it ought to be done, I will apply myself according to your custom at this time of Christmas: I will, as I said, declare unto you Christ's rule, but that shall be in Christ's cards. And whereas you are wont to celebrate Christmas in playing at cards, I intend, by God's grace, to deal unto you Christ's cards, wherein you shall perceive Christ's rule. The game that we will play at shall be called the triumph,[1] which if it be well played at, he that dealeth shall win; the players shall likewise win; and the standers and lookers upon shall do the same; insomuch that there is no man that is willing to play at this triumph with these cards, but they shall be all winners, and no losers.

Let therefore every christian man and woman play at these cards, that they may have and obtain the triumph: you must mark also that the triumph must apply to fetch home unto him all the other cards, whatsoever suit they be of. Now then, take ye this first card, which must appear and be shewed unto you as followeth: you have heard what was spoken to men of the old law, 'Thou shalt not kill; whosoever shall kill shall be in danger of judgment: but I say unto you' of the new law, saith Christ, 'that whosoever is angry with his neighbour, shall be in danger of judgment; and whosoever shall say unto his neighbour, "Raca," that is to say brainless,' or any other like

---

1 This game was something like the modern game of *Whist*. The cards, however, were not all dealt out; and the dealer had an advantage in being allowed to reject such cards from his hands as he thought proper, and take others in their stead from the undealt stock.

word of rebuking, 'shall be in danger of council; and whosoever shall say unto his neighbour, "Fool," shall be in danger of hell-fire.' This card was made and spoken by Christ, as appeareth in the fifth chapter of St Matthew.

Now it must be noted, that whosoever shall play with this card, must first, before they play with it, know the strength and virtue of the same: wherefore you must well note and mark terms, how they be spoken, and to what purpose. Let us therefore read it once or twice, that we may be the better acquainted with it.

Now behold and see, this card is divided into four parts: the first part is one of the commandments that was given unto Moses in the old law, before the coming of Christ; which commandment we of the new law be bound to observe and keep, and it is one of our commandments. The other three parts spoken by Christ be nothing else but expositions unto the first part of this commandment: for in very effect all these four parts be but one commandment, that is to say, 'Thou shalt not kill.' Yet nevertheless, the last three parts do shew unto thee how many ways thou mayest kill thy neighbour contrary to this commandment: yet, for all Christ's exposition in the three last parts of this card, the terms be not open enough to thee that dost read and hear them spoken. No doubt, the Jews understood Christ well enough, when he spake to them these three last sentences; for he spake unto them in their own natural terms and tongue. Wherefore, seeing that these terms were natural terms of the Jews, it shall be necessary to expound them, and compare them unto some like terms of our natural speech, that we in like manner may understand Christ as well as the Jews did. We will begin first with the first part of this card, and then after, with the other three parts. You must therefore understand that the Jews and the Pharisees of the old law, to whom this first part, this commandment, 'Thou shalt not kill', was spoken, thought it sufficient and enough for their discharge, not to kill with any manner of material weapon, as sword, dagger, or with any such weapon; and they thought it no great fault whatsoever they said or did by their neighbours, so that they did not harm or meddle with their corporal bodies: which was a false opinion in them, as prove well the three last other sentences following the first part of this card.

Now, as touching the three other sentences, you must note and take heed, what difference is between these three manner of offences: to be angry with your neighbour; to call your neighbour 'brainless', or any such word of disdain; or to call your neighbour 'fool'. Whether these three manner of offences be of themselves more grievous one than the other, it is to be opened unto you. Truly, as they be of themselves divers offences, so they kill adversely, one more than the other; as you shall perceive by the first of these three, and so forth. A man which conceiveth against his neighbour or brother ire or wrath in his mind, by some manner of occasion given unto him, although he be angry in his mind against his said neighbour, he will peradventure express his ire by no manner of sign, either in word or deed: yet nevertheless he offendeth against God, and breaketh this commandment in killing his own soul; and is therefore 'in danger of judgment'.

Now, to the second part of these three: That man that is moved with ire against his neighbour, and in his ire calleth his neighbour 'brainless', or some other like word of displeasure; as a man might say in a fury, 'I shall handle thee well enough'; which words and countenances do more represent and declare ire to be in this man, than in him that was but angry, and spake no manner of word nor shewed any countenance to declare his ire. Wherefore as he that so declareth his ire either by word or countenance, offendeth more against God, so he both killeth his own soul, and doth that in him is to kill his neighbour's soul in moving him unto ire, wherein he is faulty himself; and so this man is 'in danger of council'.

Now to the third offence, and last of these three: That man that calleth his neighbour 'fool', doth more declare his angry mind toward him, than he that called his neighbour but 'brainless', or any such words moving ire: for to call a man 'fool', that word representeth more envy in a man, than 'brainless' doth. Wherefore he doth most offend, because he doth most earnestly with such words express his ire, and so he is 'in danger of hell-fire'.

8

Wherefore you may understand now, these three parts of this card be three offences, and that one is more grievous to God than the other, and that one killeth more the soul of man than the other.

Now peradventure there be some that will marvel, that Christ did not declare this commandment by some greater faults of ire, than by these which seem but small faults, as to be angry and speak nothing of it, to declare it and to call a man 'brainless', and to call his neighbour 'fool': truly these be the smallest and the least faults that belong to ire, or to killing in ire. Therefore beware how you offend in any kind of ire: seeing that the smallest be damnable to offend in, see that you offend not in the greatest. For Christ thought, if he might bring you from the smallest manner of faults, and give you warning to avoid the least, he reckoned you would not offend in the greatest and worst, as to call your neighbour thief, whoreson, whore, drab, and so forth, into more blasphemous names; which offences must needs have punishment in hell, considering how that Christ hath appointed these three small faults to have three degrees of punishment in hell, as appeareth by these three terms, judgment, council, and hell-fire. These three terms do signify nothing else but three divers punishments in hell, according to the offences. Judgment is less in degree than council, therefore it signifieth a lesser pain in hell, and it is ordained for him that is angry in his mind with his neighbour, and doth express his malice neither by word nor countenance: council is a less degree in hell than hell-fire, and is a greater degree in hell than judgment; and it is ordained for him that calleth his neighbour 'brainless', or any such word, that declareth his ire and malice: wherefore it is more pain than judgment. Hell-fire is more pain in hell, than council or judgment, and it is ordained for him that calleth his neighbour 'fool', by reason that in calling his neighbour 'fool', he declareth more his malice, in that it is an earnest word of ire: wherefore hell-fire is appointed for it; that is, the most pain of the three punishments.

Now you have heard, that to these divers offences of ire and killing be appointed punishments according to their degrees:

for look as the offence is, so shall the pain be: if the offence be great, the pain shall be according; if it be less, there shall be less pain for it. I would not now that you should think, because that here are but three degrees of punishment spoken of, that there be no more in hell. No doubt Christ spake of no more here but of these three degrees of punishment, thinking they were sufficient, enough for example, whereby we might understand, that there be as divers and many pains as there be offences: and so by these three offences, and these three punishments, all other offences and punishments may be compared with another. Yet I would satisfy your minds further in these three terms, of 'judgment, council, and hell-fire'. Whereas you might say, What was the cause that Christ declared more the pains of hell by these terms, than by any other terms? I told you afore that he knew well to whom he spake them. These terms were natural and well known amongst the Jews and the Pharisees: wherefore Christ taught them with their own terms, to the intent they might understand the better his doctrine. And these terms may be likened unto three terms which we have common and usual amongst us, that is to say, the sessions of inquirance, the sessions of deliverance, and the execution-day. Sessions of inquirance is like unto judgment; for when sessions of inquiry is, then the judges cause twelve men to give verdict of the felon's crime, whereby he shall be judged to be indicted: sessions of deliverance is much like council; for at sessions of deliverance the judges go among themselves to council, to determine sentence against the felon: execution-day is to be compared unto hell-fire; for the Jews had amongst themselves a place of execution, named 'hell-fire': and surely when a man goeth to his death, it is the greatest pain in the world. Wherefore you may see that there are degrees in these our terms, as there be in those terms.

These evil-disposed affections and sensualities in us are always contrary to the rule of our salvation. What shall we do now or imagine, to thrust down these Turks and to subdue them? It is a great ignominy and shame for a christian man to be bond and subject unto a Turk: nay, it shall not be so; we will first cast a trump in their way, and play with them at cards, who shall have the better. Let us play therefore on this fashion with this card. Whensoever it shall happen the foul passions and Turks to rise in our stomachs against our brother or neighbour, either for unkind words, injuries, or wrongs, which they have done unto us, contrary unto our mind; straightways let us call unto our remembrance, and speak this question unto ourselves, 'Who art thou?' The answer is, 'I am a christian man.' Then further we must say to ourselves, 'What requireth Christ of a christian man?' Now turn up your trump, your heart (hearts is trump, as I said before), and cast your trump, your heart, on this card; and upon this card you shall learn what Christ requireth of a christian man, – not to be angry, ne moved to ire against his neighbour, in mind, countenance, nor other ways, by word or deed. Then take up this card with your heart, and lay them together: that done, you have won the game of the Turk, whereby you have defaced and overcome him by true and lawful play. But, alas for pity! the Rhodes are won[1] and overcome by these false Turks; the strong castle Faith is decayed, so that I fear it is almost impossible to win it again.

The great occasion of the loss of this Rhodes is by reason that christian men do so daily kill their own nation, that the very true number of Christianity is decayed; which murder and killing one of another is increased specially two ways, to the utter undoing of Christendom, that is to say, by example and silence. By example, as thus: when the father, the mother, the lord, the lady, the master, the dame, be themselves overcome with these Turks, they be continual swearers, avouterers,[2] disposers to malice, never in patience, and so forth in all other vices: think you not, when the father, the mother, the master, the dame, be disposed unto vice or impatience, but that their children and servants shall incline and be disposed to the same? No doubt, as the child shall take disposition natural of the father and mother, so shall the servants apply unto the vices of their masters and dames: if the heads be false in their faculties and crafts, it is no marvel if the children, servants and apprentices

1 The capture of the Island of Rhodes by the Turks in 1523.
2 Adulterers.

11

do joy therein. This is a great and shameful manner of killing christian men, that the fathers, the mothers, the masters, and the dames, shall not alonely kill themselves, but all theirs, and all that belongeth unto them: and so this way is a great number of christian lineage murdered and spoiled.

The second manner of killing is silence. By silence also is a great number of christian men slain; which is on this fashion: although that the father and mother, master and dame, of themselves be well disposed to live according to the law of God, yet they may kill their children and servants in suffering them to do evil before their own faces, and do not use due correction according unto their offences. The master seeth his servant or apprentice take more of his neighbour than the king's laws, or the order of his faculty, doth admit him; or that he suffereth him to take more of his neighbour than he himself would be content to pay, if he were in like condition: thus doing, I say, such men kill willingly their children and servants, and shall go to hell for so doing; but also their fathers and mothers, masters and dames, shall bear them company for so suffering them.

Wherefore I exhort all true christian men and women to give good example unto your children and servants, and suffer not them by silence to offend. Every man must be in his own house, according to St Augustine's mind,[1] a bishop, not alonely giving good ensample, but teaching according to it, rebuking and punishing vice; not suffering your children and servants to forget the laws of God. You ought to see them have their belief, to know the commandments of God, to keep their holy-days, not to lose their time in idleness: if they do so, you shall all suffer pain for it, if God be true of his saying, as there is no doubt thereof. And so you may perceive that there be many a one that breaketh this card, 'Thou shalt not kill', and playeth therewith oftentime at the blind trump, whereby they be no winners, but great losers. But who be those now-a-days that can clear themselves of these manifest murders used to their children and servants? I think not the contrary, but that many have these two ways slain their own children unto their damnation; unless the

1 *City of God*, Bks I, c.9 and XIX c. 19.

great mercy of God were ready to help them when they repent there-for.

Wherefore, considering that we be so prone and ready to continue in sin, let us cast down ourselves with Mary Magdalene; and the more we bow down with her toward Christ's feet, the more we shall be afraid to rise again in sin; and the more we know and submit ourselves, the more we shall be forgiven; and the less we know and submit ourselves, the less we shall be forgiven; as appeareth by this example following:

Christ, when he was in this world amongst the Jews and Pharisees, there was a great Pharisee whose name was Simon: this Pharisee desired Christ on a time to dine with him, thinking in himself that he was able and worthy to give Christ a dinner. Christ refused not his dinner, but came unto him. In time of their dinner it chanced there came into the house a great and a common sinner named Mary Magdalene. As soon as she perceived Christ, she cast herself down, and called unto her remembrance what she was of herself, and how greatly she had offended God; whereby she conceived in Christ great love, and so came near unto him, and washed his feet with bitter tears, and shed upon his head precious ointment, thinking that by him she should be delivered from her sins. This great and proud Pharisee, seeing that Christ did accept her oblation in the best part, had great indignation against this woman, and said to himself, 'If this man Christ were a holy prophet, as he is taken for, he would not suffer this sinner to come so nigh him.' Christ, understanding the naughty mind of this Pharisee, said unto him, 'Simon, I have somewhat to say unto thee.' 'Say what you please,' quod the Pharisee. Then said Christ, 'I pray thee, tell me this: If there be a man to whom is owing twenty pound by one, and forty by another, this man to whom this money is owing, perceiving these two men be not able to pay him, he forgiveth them both: which of these two debtors ought to love this man most?' The Pharisee said, 'That man ought to love him best, that had most forgiven him.' 'Likewise,' said Christ, 'it is by this woman: she hath loved me most, therefore most is forgiven her; she hath known her sins most, whereby she hath most loved me. And thou hast least loved me, because thou hast least known thy sins: therefore, because thou hast least known thine offences, thou art least forgiven.' So this proud Pharisee had an answer to delay his pride. And think you not, but that there be amongst us a great number of these proud Pharisees, which think themselves worthy to bid Christ to dinner; which will perk, and presume to sit by Christ in the church, and have a disdain of this poor woman Magdalene, their poor neighbour, with a high, disdainous, and solemn countenance? And being always desirous to climb highest in the church, reckoning themselves more worthy to sit there than another, I fear me poor Magdalene under the board, and in the belfry, hath more forgiven of Christ than they have: for it is like that those Pharisees do less know themselves and their offences, whereby they less love God, and so they be less forgiven.

I would to God we would follow this example, and be like unto Magdalene. I doubt not but we be all Magdalenes in falling into sin and in offending: but we be not again Magdalenes in knowing ourselves, and in rising from sin. If we be the true Magdalenes, we should be as willing to forsake our sin and rise from sin, as we were willing to commit sin and to continue in it; and we then should know ourselves best, and make more perfect answer than ever we did unto this question, 'Who art thou?' to the which we might answer, that we be true christian men and women: and then, I say, you should understand, and know how you ought to play at this card, 'Thou shalt not kill', without any interruption of your deadly enemies the Turks; and so triumph at the last, by winning everlasting life in glory. Amen.

The Second Sermon, To Convocation (1536)

Filii hujus seculi, &c. – Luke xvi.8.

Christ in this saying touched the sloth and sluggishness of his, and did not allow the fraud and subtlety of others; neither was glad that it was indeed as he had said, but complained rather that it should be so: as many men speak many things, not that they ought to be so, but that they are wont to be so. Nay, this grieved Christ, that the children of this world should be of more policy than the children of light; which thing was true in Christ's time, and now in our time is most true. Who is so blind but he seeth this clearly; except perchance there be any that cannot discern the children of the world from the children of light? The children of the world conceive and bring forth more prudently; and things conceived and brought forth they nourish and conserve with much more policy than do the children of light. Which thing is as sorrowful to be said, as it seemeth absurd to be heard. When ye hear the children of the world, you understand the world as a father. For the world is father of many children, not by the first creation and work, but by imitation of love. He is not only a father, but also the son of another father. If ye know once his father, by and by ye shall know his children. For he that hath the devil to his father, must needs have devilish children. The devil is not only taken for father, but also for prince of the world, that is, of worldly folk. It is either all one thing, or else not much different, to say, children of the world, and children of the devil; according to that that Christ said to the Jews, 'Ye are of your father the devil'; where as undoubtedly he spake to children of this world. Now seeing the devil is both author and ruler of the darkness, in the which the children of this world walk, or, to say better, wander; they mortally hate both the light, and also the children of light.

15

And hereof it cometh, that the children of light never, or very seldom, lack persecution in this world, unto which the children of the world, that is, of the devil, bringeth them. And there is no man but he seeth, that these use much more policy in procuring the hurt and damage of the good, than those in defending themselves. Therefore, brethren, gather you the disposition and study of the children by the disposition and study of the fathers. Ye know this is a proverb much used: 'An evil crow, an evil egg.' Then the children of this world that are known to have so evil a father, the world, so evil a grandfather, the devil, cannot choose but be evil. Surely the first head of their ancestry was the deceitful serpent the devil, a monster monstrous above all monsters. I cannot wholly express him, I wot not what to call him, but a certain thing altogether made of the hatred of God, of mistrust in God, of lyings, deceits, perjuries, discords, manslaughters; and, to say at one word, a thing concrete, heaped up and made of all kind of mischief. But what the devil mean I to go about to describe particularly the devil's nature, when no reason, no power of man's mind can comprehend it? This alonely I can say grossly, and as in a sum, of the which all we (our hurt is the more) have experience, the devil to be a stinking sentine[1] of all vices; a foul filthy channel of all mischiefs; and that this world, his son, even a child meet to have such a parent, is not much unlike his father.

Then, this devil being such one as can never be unlike himself; lo, of Envy, his well beloved Leman,[2] he begat the World, and after left it with Discord at nurse; which World, after that it came to man's state, had of many concubines many sons. He was so fecund a father, and had gotten so many children of Lady Pride, Dame Gluttony, Mistress Avarice, Lady Lechery, and of Dame Subtlety, that now hard and scant ye may find any corner, any kind of life, where many of his children be not. In court, in cowls, in cloisters, in rochets, be they never so white; yea, where shall ye not find them? Howbeit, they that be secular and laymen, are not by and by children of the world; nor they

1 Pool of collected filth.
2 A harlot.

children of light, that are called spiritual, and of the clergy. No, no; as ye may find among the laity many children of light, so among the clergy, (how many soever we arrogate these holy titles unto us, and think them only attributed to us, *Vos estis lux mundi, peculium Christi*, &c. 'Ye are the light of the world, the chosen people of Christ, a kingly priesthood, an holy nation, and such other,') ye shall find many children of the world; because in all places the world getteth many children. Among the lay people the world ceaseth not to bring to pass, that as they be called worldly, so they are worldly indeed; driven headlong by worldly desires: insomuch that they may right well seem to have taken as well the manners as the name of their father. In the clergy, the world also hath learned a way to make of men spiritual, worldlings; yea, and there also to form worldly children, where with great pretence of holiness, and crafty colour of religion, they utterly desire to hide and cloak the name of the world, as though they were ashamed of their father; which do execrate and detest the world (being nevertheless their father) in words and outward signs, but in heart and work they coll[1] and kiss him, and in all their lives declare themselves to be his babes; insomuch that in all worldly points they far pass and surmount those that they call seculars, laymen, men of the world. The child so diligently followeth the steps of his father, is never destitute of the aid of his grandfather. These be our holy holy men, that say they are dead to the world, when no men be more lively in worldly things than some of them be. But let them be in profession and name most farthest from the world, most alienate from it; yea so far, that they may seem to have no occupying, no kindred, no affinity, nothing to do with it: yet in their life and deeds they shew themselves no bastards, but right begotten children of the world; as that which the world long sithens had by his dear wife Dame Hypocrisy, and since hath brought them up and multiplied to more than a good many; increased them too much, albeit they swear by all he-saints and she-saints too, that they know not their father, nor mother, neither the world, nor hypocrisy; as indeed they can semble and

1 French *accoler*, to hang round the neck.

dissemble all things; which thing they might learn wonderful well of their parents. I speak not of all religious men, but of those that the world hath fast knit at his girdle, even in the midst of their religion, that is, of many and more than many. For I fear, lest in all orders of men the better, I must say the greater part of them be out of order, and children of the world. Many of these might seem ingrate and unkind children, that will no better acknowledge and recognise their parents in words and outward pretence, but abrenounce and cast them off, as though they hated them as dogs and serpents. Howbeit they, in this wise, are most grateful to their parents, because they be most like them, so lively representing them in countenance and conditions, that their parents seem in them to be young again, forasmuch as they ever say one thing and think another. They shew themselves to be as sober, as temperate, as Curius[1] the Roman was, and live every day as though all their life were a shroving time. They be like their parents, I say, inasmuch as they, in following them, seem and make men believe they hate them. Thus grandfather Devil, father World, and mother Hypocrisy, have brought them up. Thus good obedient sons have borne away their parents' commandments; neither these be solitary, how religious, how mocking, how monking, I would say, soever they be.

O ye will lay this to my charge, that *monachus* and *solitarius* signifieth all one. I grant this to be so, yet these be so solitary that they be not alone, but accompanied with great flocks of fraternities. And I marvel if there be not a great sort of bishops and prelates, that are brethren germain unto these; and as a great sort, so even as right born, and world's children by as good title as they. But because I cannot speak of all, when I say prelates, I understand bishops, abbots, priors, archdeacons, deans, and other of such sort, that are now called to this convocation, as I see, to entreat here of nothing but of such matters as both appertain to the glory of Christ, and to the wealth of the people of England. Which thing I pray God they

1 Curius Dentatus – *incomptis Curium capillis* (long-haired Curius) – Horace, *Odes* I. xii. 41.

do as earnestly as they ought to do. But it is to be feared lest, as light hath many her children here, so the world hath sent some of his whelps hither: amongst the which I know there can be no concord nor unity, albeit they be in one place, in one congregation. I know there can be no agreement between these two, as long as they have minds so unlike, and so contrary affections, judgments so utterly diverse in all points. But if the children of this world be either more in number, or more prudent than the children of light, what then availeth us to have this convocation? Had it not been better we had not been called together at all? For as the children of this world be evil, so they breed and bring forth things evil; and yet there be more of them in all places, or at the least they be more politic than the children of light in their generation. And here I speak of the generation whereby they do engender, and not of that whereby they are engendered, because it should be too long to entreat how the children of light are engendered, and how they come in at the door; and how the children of the world be engendered, and come in another way. Howbeit, I think all you that be here were not engendered after one generation, neither that ye all came by your promotions after one manner: God grant that ye, engendered worldly, do not engender worldly: and as now I much pass not how ye were engendered, or by what means ye were promoted to those dignities that ye now occupy, so it be honest, good and profitable, that ye in this your consultation shall do and engender.

The end of your convocation shall shew what ye have done; the fruit that shall come of your consultation shall shew what generation ye be of. For what have ye done hitherto, I pray you, these seven years and more? What have ye engendered? What have ye brought forth? What fruit is come of your long and great assembly? What one thing that the people of England hath been the better of a hair; or you yourselves, either more accepted before God, or better discharged toward the people committed unto your cure? For that the people is better learned and taught now, than they were in time past, to whether of thee ought we to attribute it, to your industry, or to the providence of God, and the foreseeing of the king's grace? Ought we to thank you, or the king's highness? Whether stirred other first, you the king, that he might preach, or he you by his letters, that ye should preach oftener? Is it unknown, think you, how both ye and your curates were, in [a] manner, by violence enforced to let books to be made, not by you, but by profane and lay persons; to let them, I say, be sold abroad, and read for the instruction of the people? I am bold with you, but I speak Latin and not English, to the clergy, not to the laity; I speak to you being present, and not behind your backs. God is my witness, I speak whatsoever is spoken of the good-will that I bear you; God is my witness, which knoweth my heart, and compelleth me to say that I say.

Now, I pray you in God's name, what did you, so great fathers, so many, so long a season, so oft assembled together? What went you about? What would ye have brought to pass? Two things taken away – the one, that ye (which I heard) burned a dead man;[1] the other, that ye (which I felt) went about to burn one being alive: him, because he did, I cannot tell how, in his testament withstand your profit; in other points, as I have heard, a very good man; reported to be of an honest life while he lived, full of good works, good both to the clergy, and also to the laity: this other,[2] which truly never hurt any of you, ye would have raked in the coals, because he would not subscribe to certain articles that took away the supremacy of the king: – take away these two noble acts, and there is nothing else left that ye went about, that I know, saving that I now remember, that somewhat ye attempted against Erasmus,[3] albeit as yet nothing is come to light. Ye have oft sat in consultation, but what have ye done? Ye have had many things in deliberation, but what one is put forth, whereby either Christ is more glorified, or else Christ's people made more holy? I appeal to your own conscience. How chanced this? How came it thus? Because there were no children of light, no children of God

---

1 The body of William Tracy, posthumously declared a heretic on the basis of statements in his will.
2 Latimer himself.
3 An allusion to the attempt of Dr Standish (1520) to fasten the charge of heresy on Erasmus.

amongst you, which, setting the world at nought, would study to illustrate the glory of God, and thereby shew themselves children of light? I think not so, certainly I think not so. God forbid, that all you, which were gathered together under the pretence of light, should be children of the world! Then why happened this? Why, I pray you? Perchance, either because the children of the world were more in number in this your congregation, as it oft happeneth, or at the least of more policy than the children of light in their generation: whereby it might very soon be brought to pass, that these were much more stronger in gendering the evil, than these in producing the good. The children of light have policy, but it is like the policy of the serpent, and is joined with doveish simplicity. They engender nothing but simply, faithfully, and plainly, even so doing all that they do. And therefore they may with more facility be cumbered in their engendering, and be the more ready to take injuries. But the children of this world have worldly policy, foxly craft, lion-like cruelty, power to do hurt, more than either *aspis* or *basiliscus*, engendering and doing all things fraudulently, deceitfully, guilefully: which as Nimrods and such sturdy and stout hunters, being full of simulation and dissimulation before the Lord, deceive the children of light, and cumber them easily. Hunters go not forth in every man's sight, but do their affairs closely, and with use of guile and deceit wax every day more craftier than other.

The children of this world be like crafty hunters; they be misnamed children of light, forasmuch as they so hate light, and so study to do the works of darkness. If they were the children of light, they would not love darkness. It is no marvel that they go about to keep other in darkness, seeing they be in darkness, from top to toe overwhelmed with darkness, darker than is the darkness of hell. Wherefore it is well done in all orders of men, but especial in the order of prelates, to put a difference between children of light and children of the world, because great deceit ariseth in taking the one for the other. Great imposture cometh, when they that the common people take for the light, go about to take the sun and the light out of the world. But these be easily known, both by the diversity of minds, and also their armours.

For whereas the children of light are thus minded, that they seek their adversaries' health, wealth, and profit, with loss of their own commodities, and oft times with jeopardy of their life; the children of the world, contrariwise, have such stomachs, that they will sooner see them dead that doth them good, than sustain any loss of temporal things. The armour of the children of light are, first, the word of God, which they ever set forth, and with all diligence put it abroad, that, as much as in them lieth, it may bring forth fruit: after this, patience and prayer, with the which in all adversities the Lord comforteth them. Other things they commit to God, unto whom they leave all revengement. The armour of the children of the world are, sometime frauds and deceits, sometime lies and money: by the first they make their dreams, their graditions; by the second they stablish and confirm their dreams, be they never so absurd, never so against scripture, honesty, or reason. And if any man resist them, even with these weapons they procure to slay him. Thus they bought Christ's death, the very light itself, and obscured him after his death: thus they buy every day the children of light, and obscure them, and shall so do, until the world be at an end. So that it may be ever true, that Christ said: 'The children of the world be wiser, &c.'

These worldlings pull down the lively faith, and full confidence that men have in Christ, and set up another faith, another confidence, of their own making: the children of light contrary. These worldlings set little by such works as God hath prepared for our salvation, but they extol traditions and works of their own invention: the children of light contrary. The worldlings, if they spy profit, gains, or lucre in any thing, be it never such a trifle, be it never so pernicious, they preach it to the people, (if they preach at any time,) and these things they defend with tooth and nail. They can scarce disallow the abuses of these, albeit they be intolerable, lest in disallowing the abuse they lose part of their profit. The children of the light contrary, put all things in their degree, best highest, next next, the worst lowest. They extol things necessary, christian, and commanded of God. They pull down will-works feigned by men, and put them in their place. The abuses of all things they earnestly rebuke. But yet these things be so done on both parties, and so they both do gender, that the children of the world shew themselves wiser than the children of the light, and that frauds and deceits, lies and money, seem evermore to have the upper hand. I hold my peace; I will not say how fat feasts, and jolly banquets, be jolly instruments to set forth worldly matters withal. Neither the children of the world be only wiser than the children of light, but are also some of them among themselves much wiser than the other in their generation. For albeit, as touching the end, the generation of them is all is one; yet in this same generation some of them have more craftily engendered than the other of their fellows.

For what a thing was that, that once every hundred year was brought forth in Rome of the children of this world, and with how much policy it was made, ye heard at Paul's Cross in the beginning of the last parliament: how some brought forth canonizations, some expectations,[1] some pluralities and unions, some tot-quots[2] and dispensations, some pardons, and these of wonderful variety, some stationaries,[3] some jubilaries,[4] some poculiaries[5] for drinkers, some manuaries[6] for handlers of

---

1 *Gratiæ expectivæ*, or certain papal instruments by which benefices, not yet vacant, were prospectively made over to purchasers. Many laws were enacted in England against this abuse.
2 An abbreviation of *totiens quotiens* in papal documents and grants, by which indulgences (expiating sins) were awarded in proportion to church attendance.
3 During a time of pestilence Gregory I appointed certain litanies and masses to be sung in the principal churches in Rome on certain fixed days for the remission of sins. These solemnities were continued ever afterwards on stated occasions, and called *Stations*.
4 Pope Boniface VIII instituted the first *jubliee* at Rome in the year 1300, promising plenary remission of sins to all who should visit Rome at that festival. These jubilees were at first ordered to be celebrated once in 100 years; but Clement VI shortened that period to 50 years; Paul II (who was followed in this by Sextus IV) reduced the interval to 25 years; whilst Alexander VI, to increase his revenue, assigned jubilees to be held in provinces and countries at a distance from Rome as well as in Rome itself.
5 Consecrated drinking-vessels.
6 Consecrated gloves.

relicks, some pedaries[1] for pilgrims, some oscularies[2] for kissers; some of them engendered one, some other such fetures,[3] and every one in that he was delivered of, was excellent politic, wise; yea, so wise, that with their wisdom they had almost made all the world fools.

But yet they that begot and brought forth that our old ancient purgatory pick-purse; that that was swaged and cooled with a Franciscan's cowl, put upon a dead man's back, to the fourth part of his sins; that that was utterly to be spoiled, and of none other but of our most prudent lord Pope, and of him as oft as him listed; that satisfactory, that missal, that scalary:[4] they, I say, that were the wise fathers and genitors of this purgatory, were in my mind the wisest of all their generation, and so far pass the children of light, and also the rest of their company, that they both are but fools, if ye compare them with these. It was a pleasant fiction, and from the beginning so profitable to the feigners of it, that almost, I dare boldly say, there hath been no emperor that hath gotten more by taxes and tallages of them that were alive, than these, the very and right-begotten sons of the world, got by dead men's tributes and gifts. If there be some in England, that would this sweeting of the world to be with no less policy kept still than it was born and brought forth in Rome, who then can accuse Christ of lying? No, no; as it hath been ever true, so it shall be, that the children of the world be much wiser, not only in making their things, but also in conserving them. I wot not what it is, but somewhat it is I wot, that some men be so loth to see the abuse of this monster, purgatory, which abuse is more than abominable: as who should say, there is none abuse in it, or else as though there can be none in it. They may seem heartily to love the old thing, that thus earnestly endeavour

---

1 Consecrated sandals.
2 Consecrated tablets on which were representations of Christ, the Virgin Mary, or some saint. Virtues, pardons, merits, &c. of various kinds were supposed to be derived from the purchase and use of these several consecrated articles, eg. the *pardon-bowl* mentioned by Latimer in his sermon 'Of the Plough', p. 47.
3 Fetures: births or productions.
4 Masses-satisfactory, – soul-masses, – masses of *scala cœli*.

them to restore him his old name. They would not set an hair by the name, but for the thing. They be not so ignorant, (no, they be crafty,) but that they know if the name come again, the thing will come after. Thereby it ariseth, that some men make their cracks, that they, maugre all men's heads, have found purgatory. I cannot tell what is found. This, to pray for dead folks, this is not found, for it was never lost. How can that be found that was not lost? O subtle finders, that can find things, if God will, ere they be lost! For that cowlish deliverance, their scalary loosings, their papal spoliations, and other such their figments, they cannot find. No, these be so lost, as they themselves grant, that though they seek them never so diligently, yet they shall not find them, except perchance they hope to see them come in again with their names; and that then money-gathering may return again, and deceit walk about the country, and so stablish their kingdom in all kingdoms. But to what end this chiding between the children of the world and the children of light will come, only he knoweth that once shall judge them both.

Now, to make haste and to come somewhat nigher the end. Go ye to, good brethren and fathers, for the love of God, go ye to; and seeing we are here assembled, let us do something whereby we may be known to be the children of light. Let us do somewhat, lest we, which hitherto have been judged children of the world, seem even still to be so. All men call us prelates: then, seeing we be in council, let us so order ourselves, that we be prelates in honour and dignity; so we may be prelates in holiness, benevolence, diligence, and sincerity. All men know that we be here gathered, and with most fervent desire they anheale,[1] breathe, and gape for the fruit of our convocation: as our acts shall be, so they shall name us: so that now it lieth in us, whether we will be called children of the world, or children of light.

Wherefore lift up your heads, brethren, and look about with your eyes, spy what things are to be reformed in the church of England. Is it so hard, is it so great a matter for you to see many

1 Are breathlessly anxious (*anhelare*).

abuses in the clergy, many in the laity? What is done in the Arches?[1] Nothing to be amended? What do they there? Do they evermore rid the people's business and matters, or cumber and ruffle them? Do they evermore correct vice, or else defend it, sometime being well corrected in other places? How many sentences be given there in time, as they ought to be? If men say truth, how many without bribes? Or if all things be well done there, what do men in bishops' Consistories?[2] shall you often see the punishments assigned by the laws executed, or else money-redemptions used in their stead? How think you by the ceremonies that are in England, oft-times, with no little offence of weak consciences, contemned; more oftener with superstition so defiled, and so depraved, that you may doubt whether it were better some of them to tarry still, or utterly to take them away? Have not our forefathers complained of the ceremonies, of the superstition, and estimation of them?

Do ye see nothing in our holidays? of the which very few were made at the first, and they to set forth goodness, virtue, and honesty: but sithens, in some places, there is neither mean nor measure in making new holidays, as who should say, this one thing is serving of God, to make this law, that no man may work. But what doth the people on these holidays? Do they give themselves to godliness, or else ungodliness? See ye nothing, brethren? If you see not, yet God seeth. God seeth all the whole holidays to be spent miserably in drunkenness, in glossing, in strife, in envy, in dancing, dicing, idleness, and gluttony. He seeth all this, and threateneth punishment for it. He seeth it, which neither is deceived in seeing, nor deceiveth when he threateneth.

Thus men serve the devil; for God is not thus served, albeit ye say ye serve God. No, the devil hath more service done unto him on one holiday, than on many working days. Let all these

1 The chief and most ancient Consistory court belonging to the archbishop of Canterbury. The name is derived from the Court having been formerly held in the church of St Mary *le bow* (*S. Maria de Arcubus*).
2 All bishops have a Consistory court for the trial of ecclesiastical causes arising within their respective dioceses.

abuses be counted as nothing, who is he that is not sorry, to see in so many holidays rich and wealthy persons to flow in delicates, and men that live by their travail, poor men, to lack necessary meat and drink for their wives and their children, and that they cannot labour upon the holidays, except they will be cited, and brought before our Officials? Were it not the office of good prelates to consult upon these matters, and to seek some remedy for them? Ye shall see, my brethren, ye shall see once, what will come of this our winking.

What think ye of these images that are had more than their fellows in reputation;[1] that are gone unto with such labour and weariness of the body, frequented with such our cost, sought out and visited with such confidence? What say ye by these images, that are so famous, so noble, so noted, being of them so many and so divers in England? Do you think that this preferring of picture to picture, image to image, is the right use, and not rather the abuse, of images? But you will say to me, Why make ye all these interrogations? and why, in these your demands, do you let and withdraw the good devotion of the people? Be not all things well done, that are done with good intent, when they be profitable to us? So, surely covetousness both thinketh and speaketh. Were it not better for us, more for estimation, more meeter for men in our places, to cut away a piece of this our profit, if we will not cut away all, than to wink at such ungodliness, and so long to wink for a little lucre; specially if it be ungodliness, and also seem unto you ungodliness? These be two things, so oft to seek mere images, and sometime to visit the relicks of saints. And yet, as in those there may be much ungodliness committed, so there may here some superstition be hid, if that sometime we chance to visit pigs' bones instead of saints' relicks, as in time past it hath chanced, I had almost said, in England. Then this is too great a blindness, a darkness too sensible, that there should be so commended in sermons of some men, and preached to be done

1 'They will make comparisons betweene our lady of Ippiswitch and our ladie of Walsingham: as wening that one image more of power than the other.' – Sir Thomas More.

after such manner, as though they could not be evil done; which, notwithstanding, are such, that neither God nor man commandeth them to be done. No, rather, men commanded them either not to be done at all, or else more slowlier and seldomer to be done, forasmuch as our ancestors made this constitution: 'We command the priests, that they oft admonish the people, and in especial women, that they make no vows but after long deliberation, consent of their husbands, and counsel of the priest.'[1] The church of England in time past made this constitution. What saw they that made this decree? They saw the intolerable abuses of images. They saw the perils that might ensue of going on pilgrimage. They saw the superstitious difference that men made between image and image. Surely, somewhat they saw. The constitution is so made, that in manner it taketh away all such pilgrimages. For it so plucketh away the abuse of them, that it leaveth either none, or else seldom use of them. For they that restrain making vows for going of pilgrimage, restrain also pilgrimage; seeing that for the most part it is seen that few go on pilgrimage but vow-makers, and such as by promise bind themselves to go. And when, I pray you, should a man's wife go on pilgrimage, if she went not before she had well debated the matter with herself, and obtained the consent of her husband, being a wise man, and were also counselled by a learned priest so to do? When should she go far off to these famous images? For this the common people of England think to be going on pilgrimage: to go to some dead and notable image out of town, that is to say, far from their house. Now if your forefathers made this constitution, and yet thereby did nothing, the abuses every day more and more increased, what is left for you to do? Brethren and fathers, if ye purpose to do any thing, what should ye sooner do, than to take utterly away these deceitful and juggling images; or else, if ye know any other mean to put away abuses, to shew it, if ye intend to remove abuses? Methink it should be grateful and pleasant to you to mark the earnest mind of your

1 The constitution alluded to is attributed to Edmund, archbishop of Canterbury in the year 1236.

forefathers, and to look upon their desire where they say in their constitution, 'We *command* you', and not, 'We *counsel* you.' How have we been so long a-cold, so long slack in setting forth so wholesome a precept of the church of England, where we be so hot in all things that have any gains in them, albeit they be neither commanded us, nor yet given us by counsel; as though we have lever the abuse of things should tarry still than, it taken away, lose our profit? To let pass the solemn and nocturnal bacchanals, the prescript miracles, that are done upon certain days in the west part of England, who hath not heard? I think ye have heard of St Blesis's[1] heart which is at Malverne, and of St Algar's[2] bones, how long they deluded the people: I am afraid, to the loss of many souls. Whereby men may well conjecture, that all about in this realm there is plenty of such juggling deceits. And yet hitherto ye have sought no remedy. But even still the miserable people are suffered to take the false miracles for the true, and to lie still asleep in all kind of superstition. God have mercy upon us!

Last of all, how think you of matrimony? Is all well here? What of baptism? Shall we evermore in ministering of it speak Latin, and not in English rather, that the people may know what is said and done?

What think ye of these mass-priests, and of the masses themselves? What say ye? Be all things here so without abuses, that nothing ought to be amended? Your forefathers saw somewhat, which made this constitution[3] against the venality and sale of masses, that, under pain of suspending, no priest should sell his saying of tricennals[4] or

1   Probably St Blaise.
2   Probably Algar the father of Fremond, the latter being a Mercian saint.
3   The allusion seems to be to the mandate of Simon Islip, archbishop of Canterbury (1350).
4   Tricennals or *Trentals* – 'a trentall of masses:…Three Masses of the Nativity of our Lord: Three Masses of the Epiphany: Three of the Purification of our Lady: Three of the Annunciation of our Lady: Three of the Resurrection: Three of the Ascension: Three of Pentecost: Three of the Trinity: Three of the Assumption of our Lady; and of her nativity.'

annals.[1] What saw they, that made this constitution? What priests saw they? What manner of masses saw they, trow ye? But at the last, what became of so good a constitution? God have mercy upon us! If there be nothing to be amended abroad, concerning the whole, let every one of us make one better: if there be neither abroad nor at home any thing to be amended or redressed, my lords, be ye of good cheer, be merry; and at the least, because we have nothing else to do, let us reason the matter how we may be richer. Let us fall to some pleasant communication; after let us go home, even as good as we came hither, that is, right-begotten children of the world, and utterly worldlings. And while we live here, let us all make bone cheer.[2] For after this life there is small pleasure, little mirth for us to hope for; if now there be nothing to be changed in our fashions. Let us say, not as St Peter did, 'Our end approacheth nigh', this is an heavy hearing; but let us say as the evil servant said, 'It will be long ere my master come.' This is pleasant. Let us beat our fellows: let us eat and drink with drunkards. Surely, as oft as we do not take away the abuse of things, so oft we beat our fellows. As oft as we give not the people their true food, so oft we beat our fellows. As oft as we let them die in superstition, so oft we beat them. To be short, as oft as we blind lead them blind, so oft we beat, and grievously beat our fellows. When we welter in pleasures and idleness, then we eat and drink with drunkards. But God will come, God will come, he will not tarry long away. He will come upon such a day as we nothing look for him, and at such hour as we know not. He will come and cut us in pieces. He will reward us as he doth the hypocrites. He will set us where wailing shall be, my brethren; where gnashing of teeth shall be, my brethren. And let here be the end of our tragedy, if ye will. These be the delicate dishes prepared for the world's well-beloved children. These be the wafers and junkets provided for worldly prelates, – wailing and gnashing

1 A yearly mass said for a certain dead person, upon the anniversary day of his death. A mass said for the soul of a deceased person every day for a whole year, was also called an Annal.
2 *bonne chère.*

of teeth. Can there be any mirth, where these two courses last all the feast? Here we laugh, there we shall weep. Our teeth make merry here, ever dashing in delicates; there we shall be torn with teeth, and do nothing but gnash and grind our own. To what end have we now excelled other in policy? What have we brought forth at the last? Ye see, brethren, what sorrow, what punishment is provided for you, if ye be worldlings. If ye will not thus be vexed, be ye not the children of the world. If ye will not be children of the world, be not stricken with the love of worldly things; lean not upon them. If ye will not die eternally, live not worldly. Come, go to; leave the love of your profit; study for the glory and profit of Christ; seek in your consultations such things as pertain to Christ, and bring forth at the last somewhat that may please Christ. Feed ye tenderly, with all diligence, the flock of Christ. Preach truly the word of God. Love the light, walk in the light, and so be ye the children of light while ye are in this world, that ye may shine in the world that is to come bright as the sun, with the Father, the Son, and the Holy Ghost; to whom be all honour, praise, and glory. *Amen.*

The Sermon on the Plough (1548)

Quæcunque scripta sunt ad nostram doctrinam scripta sunt –
Rom. xv. 4.

'All things which are written, are written for our erudition and
knowledge. All things that are written in God's book, in the
Bible book, in the book of the holy scripture, are written to be
our doctrine.'

I told you in my first sermon, honourable audience, that I
purposed to declare unto you two things. The one, what seed
should be sown in God's field, in God's plough land; and the
other, who should be the sowers: that is to say, what doctrine
is to be taught in Christ's church and congregation, and what
men should be the teachers and preachers of it. The first part I
have told you in the three sermons past, in which I have assayed
to set forth my plough, to prove what I could do. And now I
shall tell you who be the ploughers: for God's word is a seed to
be sown in God's field, that is, the faithful congregation, and
the preacher is the sower. And it is in the gospel: '*Exivit qui
seminat seminare semen suum*; 'He that soweth, the husbandman,
the ploughman, went forth to sow his seed.' So that a preacher
is resembled to a ploughman, as it is in another place: *Nemo
admota aratro manu, et a tergo respiciens, aptus est regno Dei*. 'No
man that putteth his hand to the plough, and looketh back, is
apt for the kingdom of God.' That is to say, let no preacher be
negligent in doing his office. Albeit this is one of the places that
hath been racked,[1] as I told you of racking scriptures. And I have
been one of them myself that hath racked it, I cry God mercy
for it; and have been one of them that have believed and

---

1 Referring to the Roman Catholic application of this passage to
monastic vows.

expounded it against religious persons that would forsake their order which they had professed, and would go out of their cloister: whereas indeed it toucheth not monkery, nor maketh anything at all for any such matter; but it is directly spoken of diligent preaching of the word of God.

For preaching of the gospel is one of God's plough-works, and the preacher is one of God's ploughmen. Ye may not be offended with my similitude, in that I compare preaching to the labour and work of ploughing, and the preacher to a plough-man: ye may not be offended with this my similitude; for I have been slandered of some persons for such things. It hath been said of me, 'Oh Latimer! nay, as for him, I will never believe him while I live, nor never trust him; for he likened our blessed lady to a saffron-bag':[1] where indeed I never used that similitude. But it was, as I have said unto you before now, according to that which Peter saw before in the spirit of prophecy, and said, that there should come after men *per quos via veritatis maledictis afficeratur*; there should come fellows 'by whom the way of truth should be evil spoken of, and slandered.' But in case I had used this similitude, it had not been to be reproved, but might have been without reproach. For I might have said thus: as the saffron-bag that hath been full of saffron, or hath had saffron in it, doth ever after savour and smell of the sweet saffron that it contained; so our blessed lady, which conceived and bare Christ in her womb, did ever after resemble the manners and virtues of that precious babe that she bare. And what had our blessed lady been the worse for this? or what dishonour was this to our blessed lady? But as preachers must be wary and circumspect, that they give not any just occasion to be slandered and ill spoken of by the hearers, so must not the auditors be offended without cause. For heaven is in the gospel likened to a mustard-seed: it is compared also to a piece of leaven; and as Christ saith, that at the last day he will come like a thief: and what dishonour is this to God? or

1 Among the 'erroneous opinions complained of in his convocation', 1536 was 'that our lady was no better than another woman, and like a bag of pepper or saffron when the spice is out'.

what derogation is this to heaven? Ye may not then, I say, be offended with my similitude, for because I liken preaching to a ploughman's labour, and a prelate to a ploughman. But now you will ask me, whom I call a prelate? A prelate is that man, whatsoever he be, that hath a flock to be taught of him; whosoever hath any spiritual charge in the faithful congregation, and whosoever he be that hath cure of souls. And well may the preacher and the ploughman be likened together: first, for their labour of all seasons of the year; for there is no time of the year in which the ploughman hath not some special work to do: as in my country in Leicestershire, the ploughman hath a time to set forth, and to assay his plough, and other times for other necessary works to be done. And then they also may be likened together for the diversity of works and variety of offices that they have to do. For as the ploughman first setteth forth his plough, and then tilleth his land, and breaketh it in furrows, and sometime ridgeth it up again; and at another time harroweth it and clotteth it, and sometime dungeth it and hedgeth it, diggeth it and weedeth it, purgeth and maketh it clean: so the prelate, the preacher, hath many diverse offices to do. He hath first a busy work to bring his parishioners to a right faith, as Paul calleth it, and not a swerving faith; but to a faith that embraceth Christ, and trusteth to his merits; a lively faith, a justifying faith; a faith that maketh a man righteous, without respect of works: as ye have it very well declared and set forth in the Homily.[1] He hath then a busy work, I say, to bring his flock to a right faith, and then to confirm them in the same faith: now casting them down with the law, and with threatenings of God for sin; now ridging them up again with the gospel, and with the promises of God's favour: now weeding them, by telling them their faults, and making them forsake sin; now clotting them, by breaking their stony hearts, and by making them supplehearted, and making them to have hearts of flesh; that is, soft hearts, and apt for doctrine to enter in: now teaching to know God rightly, and to know their duty to God and their neighbours: now exhorting them, when they know their duty, that they do it, and be

1 'Of a true and lively faith.'

diligent in it; so that they have a continual work to do. Great is their business, and therefore great should be their hire. They have great labours, and therefore they ought to have good livings, that they may commodiously feed their flock; for the preaching of the word of God unto the people is called meat: scripture calleth it meat; not strawberries,[1] that come but once a year, and tarry not long, but are soon gone: but it is meat, it is no dainties. The people must have meat that must be familiar and continual, and daily given unto them to feed upon. Many make a strawberry of it, ministering it but once a year; but such do not the office of good prelates. For Christ saith, *Quis putas est servus prudens et fidelis? Qui dat cibum in tempore.* 'Who think you is a wise and a faithful servant? He that giveth meat in due time.' So that he must at all times convenient preach diligently: therefore saith he, 'Who trow ye is a faithful servant?' He speaketh it as though it were a rare thing to find such a one, and as though he should say, there be but a few of them to find in the world. And how few of them there be throughout this realm that give meat to their flock as they should do, the Visitors can best tell. Too few, too few; the more is the pity, and never so few as now.

By this, then, it appeareth that a prelate, or any that hath cure of soul, must diligently and substantially work and labour. Therefore saith Paul to Timothy, *Qui episcopatum desiderat, hic bonum opus desiderat:* 'He that desireth to have the office of a bishop, or a prelate, that man desireth a good work.' Then if it be a good work, it is work; ye can make but a work of it. It is God's work, God's plough, and that plough God would have still going. Such then as loiter and live idly, are not good prelates, or ministers. And of such as do not preach and teach, nor do their duties, God saith by his prophet Jeremy, *Maledictus qui facit opus Dei fradulenter;* 'Cursed be the man that doth the work of God fraudulently, guilefully or deceitfully': some books have it *negligenter,* 'negligently or slackly'. How many

---

1 This expression, which Latimer made use of to describe the non-residents of his day, who only visited their cures once a year, became proverbial.

such prelates, how many such bishops, Lord, for thy mercy, are there now in England! And what shall we in this case do? shall we company with them? O Lord, for thy mercy! shall we not company with them? O Lord, whither shall we flee from them? But 'cursed be he that doth the work of God negligently or guilefully'. A sore word for them that are negligent in discharging their office, or have done it fraudulently; for that is the thing that maketh the people ill.

But true it must be that Christ saith, *Multi sunt vocati, pauci vero electi*: 'Many are called, but few are chosen.' Here have I an occasion by the way somewhat to say unto you; yea, for the place I alleged unto you before out of Jeremy, the forty-eighth chapter. And it was spoken of a spiritual work of God, a work that was commanded to be done; and it was of shedding blood, and of destroying the cities of Moab. For, saith he, 'Cursed be he that keepeth back his sword from shedding of blood.' As Saul, when he kept back the sword from shedding of blood at what time he was sent against Amaleck, was refused of God for being disobedient to God's commandment, in that he spared Agag the king. So that that place of the prophet was spoken of them that went to the destruction of the cities of Moab, among the which there was one called Nebo, which was much reproved for idolatry, superstition, pride, avarice, cruelty, tyranny, and for hardness of heart; and for these sins was plagued of God and destroyed.

Now what shall we say of these rich citizens of London? What shall I say of them? Shall I call them proud men of London, malicious men of London, merciless men of London? No, no, I may not say so; they will be offended with me then. Yet must I speak. For is there not reigning in London as much pride, as much covetousness, as much cruelty, as much oppression, and as much superstition, as was in Nebo? Yes, I think, and much more too. Therefore I say, repent, O London; repent, repent. Thou hearest thy faults told thee, amend them, amend them. I think, if Nebo had had the preaching that thou hast, they would have converted. And, you rulers and officers, be wise and circumspect, look to your charge, and see you do your duties; and rather be glad to amend your ill living than to be angry when you are warned or told of your fault. What ado was there made in London at a certain man, because he said, (and indeed at that time on a just cause,) 'Burgesses!' quoth he, 'nay, Butterflies.' Lord, what ado there was for that word! And yet would God they were no worse than butterflies! Butterflies do but their nature: the butterfly is not covetous, is not greedy of other men's goods; is not full of envy and hatred, is not malicious, is not cruel, is not merciless. The butterfly glorieth not in her own deeds, nor preferreth the traditions of men before God's word; it committeth not idolatry, nor worshippeth false gods. But London cannot abide to be rebuked; such is the nature of man. If they be pricked, they will kick; if they be rubbed on the gall, they will wince; but yet they will not amend their faults, they will not be ill spoken of. But how shall I speak well of them? If you could be content to receive and follow the word of God, and favour good preachers, if you could bear to be told of your faults, if you could amend when you hear of them, if you would be glad to reform that is amiss; if I might see any such inclination in you, that you would leave to be merciless, and begin to be charitable, I would then hope well of you, I would then speak well of you. But London was never so ill as it is now. In times past men were full of pity and compassion, but now there is no pity; for in London their brother shall die in the streets for cold, he shall lie sick at the door between stock and stock, I cannot tell what to call it, and perish there for hunger: was there ever more unmercifulness in Nebo? I think not. In times past, when any rich man died in London, they were wont to help the poor scholars of the Universities with exhibition. When any man died, they would bequeath great sums of money toward the relief of the poor. When I was a scholar in Cambridge myself, I heard very good report of London, and knew many that had relief of the rich men of London: but now I can hear no such good report, and yet I inquire of it, and hearken for it; but now charity is waxen cold, none helpeth the scholar, nor yet the poor. And in those days, what did they when they helped the scholars? Marry, they maintained and gave them livings that were very papists, and professed the pope's doctrine: and now that the knowledge of

God's word is brought to light, and many earnestly study and labour to set it forth, now almost no man helpeth to maintain them.

Oh London, London! repent, repent; for I think God is more displeased with London than ever he was with the city of Nebo. Repent therefore, repent, London, and remember that the same God liveth now that punished Nebo, even the same God, and none other; and he will punish sin as well now as he did then: and he will punish the iniquity of London, as well as he did then of Nebo. Amend therefore. And ye that be prelates, look well to your office; for right prelating is busy labouring, and not lording. Therefore preach and teach, and let your plough be doing. Ye lords, I say, that live like loiterers, look well to your office; the plough is your office and charge. If you live idle and loiter, you do not your duty, you follow not your vocation: let your plough therefore be going, and not cease, that the ground may bring forth fruit.

But now methinketh I hear one say unto me: Wot ye what you say? Is it a work? Is it a labour? How then hath it happened that we have had so many hundred years so many unpreaching prelates, lording loiterers, and idle ministers? Ye would have me here to make answer, and to shew the cause thereof. Nay, this land is not for me to plough; it is too stony, too thorny, too hard for me to plough. They have so many things that make for them, so many things to lay for themselves, that it is not for my weak team to plough them. They have to lay for themselves long customs, ceremonies and authority, placing in parliament, and many things more. And I fear me this land is not yet ripe to be ploughed: for, as the saying is, it lacketh weathering: this gear lacketh weathering; at least way it is not for me to plough. For what shall I look for among thorns, but pricking and scratching? What among stones, but stumbling? What (I had almost said) among serpents, but stinging? But this much I dare say, that since lording and loitering hath come up, preaching hath come down, contrary to the apostles' times: for they preached and lorded not, and now they lord and preach not. For they that be lords will ill go to plough: it is not meet office for them; it is not seeming for their estate. Thus came up lording

38

loiterers: thus crept in unpreaching prelates; and so have they long continued. For how many unlearned prelates have we now at this day! And no marvel: for if the ploughmen that now be were made lords, they would clean give over ploughing; they would leave off their labour, and fall to lording outright, and let the plough stand: and then both ploughs not walking, nothing should be in the commonweal but hunger. For ever since the prelates were made lords and nobles, the plough standeth; there is no work done, the people starve. They hawk, they hunt, they card, they dice; they pastime in their prelacies with gallant gentlemen, with their dancing minions, and with their fresh companions, so that ploughing is set aside: and by their lording and loitering, preaching and ploughing is clean gone. And thus if the ploughmen of the country were as negligent in their office as prelates be, we should not long live, for lack of sustenance. And as it is necessary for to have this ploughing for the sustentation of the body, so must we have also the other for the satisfaction of the soul, or else we cannot live long ghostly. For as the body wasteth and consumeth away for lack of bodily meat, so doth the soul pine away for default of ghostly meat. But there be two kinds of inclosing, to let or hinder both these kinds of ploughing; the one is an inclosing to let or hinder the bodily ploughing, and the other to let or hinder the holiday-ploughing, the church-ploughing.

The bodily ploughing is taken in and inclosed through singular commodity. For what man will let go, or diminish his private commodity for a commonwealth? And who will sustain any damage for the respect of a public commodity? The other plough also no man is diligent to set forward, nor no man will hearken to it. But to hinder and let it all men's ears are open; yea, and a great many of this kind of ploughmen, which are very busy, and would seem to be very good workmen. I fear me some be rather mock-gospellers than faithful ploughmen. I know many myself that profess the gospel, and live nothing thereafter. I know them, and have been conversant with some of them. I know them, and (I speak it with a heavy heart) there is as little charity and good living in them as in any other;

according to that which Christ said in the gospel to the great number of people that followed him, as though they had had any earnest zeal to his doctrine, whereas indeed they had it not; *Non quia vidistis signa, sed quia comedistis de panibus.* 'Ye follow me,' saith he, 'not because ye have seen the signs and miracles that I have done; but because ye have eaten the bread, and refreshed your bodies, therefore you follow me.' So that I think many one now-a-days professeth the gospel for the living's sake, not for the love they bear to God's word. But they that will be true ploughmen must work faithfully for God's sake, for the edifying of their brethren. And as diligently as the husbandman plougheth for the sustentation of the body, so diligently must the prelates and ministers labour for the feeding of the soul: both the ploughs must still be going, as most necessary for man. And wherefore are magistrates ordained, but that the tranquility of the commonweal may be confirmed, limiting both ploughs?

But now for the fault of unpreaching prelates, methink I could guess what might be said for excusing of them. They are so troubled with lordly living, they be so placed in palaces, couched in courts, ruffling in their rents, dancing in their dominions, burdened with ambassages, pampering of their paunches, like a monk that maketh his jubilee; munching in their mangers, and moiling in their gay manors and mansions, and so troubled with loitering in their lordships, that they cannot attend it. They are otherwise occupied, some in the king's matters, some are ambassadors, some of the privy council, some to furnish the court, some are lords of the parliament, some are presidents, and comptrollers of mints.

Well, well, is this their duty? Is this their office? Is this their calling? Should we have ministers of the church to be comptrollers of the mints? Is this a meet office for a priest that hath cure of souls? Is this his charge? I would here ask one question: I would fain know who controlleth the devil at home in his parish, while he controlleth the mint? If the apostles might not leave the office of preaching to the deacons, shall one leave it for minting? I cannot tell you; but the saying is, that since priests have been minters, money hath been worse than it was before. And they say that the evilness of money hath made all things dearer. And in this behalf I must speak to England. 'Hear, my country, England,' as Paul said in his first epistle to the Corinthians, the sixth chapter; for Paul was no sitting bishop, but a walking and a preaching bishop. But when he went from them, he left there behind him the plough going still; for he wrote unto them, and rebuked them for going to law, and pleading their causes before heathen judges: 'Is there,' saith he, 'utterly among you no wise man, to be an arbitrator in matters of judgment? What, not one of all that can judge between brother and brother; but one brother goeth to law with another, and that under heathen judges? *Constituite contemptos qui sunt in ecclesia*, &c. Appoint them judges that are most abject and vile in the congregation.' Which he speaketh in rebuking them; 'For,' saith he, *ad erubescentiam vestram dico* – 'I speak it to your shame.' So, England, I speak it to thy shame: is there never a nobleman to be a lord president, but it must be a prelate? Is there never a wise man in the realm to be a comptroller of the mint? 'I speak it to your shame. I speak it to your shame.' If there be never a wise man, make a water-bearer, a tinker, a cobbler, a slave, a page, comptroller of the mint: make a mean gentleman, a groom, a yeoman, or a poor beggar, lord president.

Thus I speak, not that I would have it so; but 'to your shame', if there be never a gentleman meet nor able to be lord president. For why are not the noblemen and young gentlemen of England so brought up in knowledge of God, and in learning, that they may be able to execute offices in the commonweal? The king hath a great many of wards,[1] and I trow there is a Court of Wards: why is there not a school for the wards, as well as there is a Court for their lands? Why are they not set in schools where they may learn? Or why are they not sent to the universities, that they may be able to serve the king when they come to age? If the wards and young gentlemen were well brought up in

---

1 All minors of a certain rank were at one time regarded as wards of the crown, the rents, &c. of their estates during their nonage being paid into the royal exchequer. King Henry VIII established a Court for the management of the lands &c. of wards.

learning, and in the knowledge of God, they would not when they come to age so much give themselves to other vanities. And if the nobility be well trained in godly learning, the people would follow the same train. For truly, such as the noblemen be, such will the people be. And now, the only cause why noblemen be not made lord presidents, is because they have not been brought up in learning.

Therefore for the love of God appoint teachers and schoolmasters, you that have charge of youth; and give the teachers stipends worthy their pains, that they may bring them up on grammar, in logic, in rhetoric, in philosophy, in the civil law, and in that which I cannot leave unspoken of, the word of God. Thanks be unto God, the nobility otherwise is very well brought up in learning and godliness, the great joy and comfort of England: so that there is now good hope in the youth, that we shall another day have a flourishing commonweal, considering their godly education. Yea, and there be already noblemen enough, though not so many as I would wish, able to be lord presidents, and wise men enough for the mint. And as unmeet a thing it is for bishops to be lord presidents, or priests to be minters, as it was for the Corinthians to plead matters of variance before heathen judges. It is also a slander to the noblemen, as though they lacked wisdom and learning to be able for such offices, or else were no men of conscience, or else were not meet to be trusted, and able for such offices. And a prelate hath a charge and cure otherwise; and therefore he cannot discharge his duty and be a lord president too. For a presidentship requireth a whole man; and a bishop cannot be two men. A bishop hath his office, a flock to teach, to look unto; and therefore he cannot meddle with another office, which alone requireth a whole man: he should therefore give it over to whom it is meet, and labour in his own business; as Paul writeth to the Thessalonians, 'Let every man do his own business, and follow his calling.' Let the priest preach, and the noblemen handle the temporal matters. Moses was a marvellous man, a good man: Moses was a wonderful fellow, and did his duty, being a married man: we lack such as Moses was. Well, I would all men would look to their duty, as God hath called them, and then we should have a flourishing christian commonweal.

And now I would ask a strange question: who is the most diligentest bishop and prelate in all England, that passeth all the rest in doing his office? I can tell, for I know him who it is; I know him well. But now I think I see you listening and hearkening that I should name him. There is one that passeth all the other, and is the most diligent prelate and preacher in all England. And will ye know who it is? I will tell you: it is the devil. He is the most diligent preacher of all other; ye shall never find him unoccupied; he is ever in his parish; he keepeth residence at all times; ye shall never find him out of the way, call for him when you will he is ever at home; the diligentest preacher in all the realm; he is ever at his plough: no lording nor loitering can hinder him; he is ever applying his business, ye shall never find him idle, I warrant you. And his office is to hinder religion, to maintain superstition, to set up idolatry, to teach all kind of popery. He is ready as he can be wished for to set forth his plough; to devise as many ways as can be to deface and obscure God's glory. Where the devil is resident, and hath his plough going, there away with books, and up with candles; away with bibles, and up with beads; away with the light of the gospel, and up with the light of candles; yea, at noon-days. Where the devil is resident, that he may prevail, up with all superstition and idolatry; censing, painting of images, candles, palms, ashes, holy water, and new service of men's inventing; as though man could invent a better way to honour God with than God himself that appointed. Down with Christ's cross, up with purgatory pickpurse, up with him, the popish purgatory, I mean. Away with clothing the naked, the poor and impotent; up with decking of images, and gay garnishing of stocks and stones: up with man's traditions and his laws and down with God's traditions and his most holy word. Down with the old honour due to God, and up with the new god's honour. Let all things be done in Latin: there must be nothing but Latin, not so much as *Memento, homo, quod cinis es, et in cinerem reverteris*: 'Remember, man, that thou art ashes, and into ashes thou shalt return': which be the words that the minister speaketh unto the

43

ignorant people, when he giveth them ashes upon Ash-Wednesday; but it must be spoken in Latin: God's word may in no wise be translated into English.

Oh that our prelates would be as diligent to sow the corn of good doctrine, as Satan is to sow cockle and darnel! And this is the devilish ploughing, the which worketh to have things in Latin, and letteth the fruitful edification. But here some man will say to me, What, sir, are ye so privy of the devil's counsel, that ye know all this to be true? Truly I know him too well, and have obeyed him a little too much in condescending to some follies; and I know him as other men do, yea, that he is ever occupied, and ever busy in following his plough. I know by St Peter, which saith of him, *Sicut leo rugiens circuit quærens quem devoret*: 'He goeth about like a roaring lion, seeking whom he may devour.' I would have this text well viewed and examined, every word of it: '*Circuit*', he goeth about in every corner of his diocese; he goeth on visitation daily, he leaveth no place of his cure unvisited: he walketh round about from place to place, and ceaseth not. '*Sicut leo*', as a lion, that is, strongly, boldly, and proudly; stately and fiercely with haughty looks, with his proud countenances, with his stately braggings. '*Rugiens*', roaring; for he letteth not slip any occasion to speak or to roar out when he seeth his time. *Quærens*, he goeth about seeking, and not sleeping, as our bishops do; but he seeketh diligently, he searcheth diligently all corners, where as he may have his prey. He roveth abroad in every place of his diocess; he standeth not still, he is never at rest, but ever in hand with his plough, that it may go forward. But there was never such a preacher in England as he is. Who is able to tell his diligent preaching, which every day, and every hour, laboureth to sow cockle and darnel, that he may bring out of form, and out of estimation and room,[1] the institution of the Lord's supper and Christ's cross? For there he lost his right; for Christ said, *Nunc judicium est mundi, princeps seculi hujus ejicietur foras. Et sicut exaltavit Moses serpentem in deserto, ita exaltari oportet Filium hominis. Et cum exaltatus fuero a terra, omnia traham ad meipsum.* 'Now is the

1 Place or office.

judgment of this world, and the prince of this world shall be cast out. And as Moses did lift up the serpent in the wilderness, so must the Son of man be lift up. And when I shall be lift up from the earth, I will draw all things unto myself.' For the devil was disappointed of his purpose: for he thought all to be his own; and when he had once brought Christ to the cross, he thought all cocksure. But there lost he all reigning: for Christ said, *Omnia traham ad meipsum*: 'I will draw all things to myself.' He meaneth, drawing of man's soul to salvation. And that he said he would do *per semetipsum*, by his own self; not by any other body's sacrifice. He meant by his own sacrifice on the cross, where he offered himself for the redemption of mankind; and not the sacrifice of the mass to be offered by another. For who can offer him but himself? He was both the offerer and the offering. And this is the prick, this is the mark at the which the devil shooteth, to evacuate the cross of Christ, and to mingle the institution of the Lord's supper; the which although he cannot bring to pass, yet he goeth about by his sleights and subtil means to frustrate the same; and these fifteen hundred years he hath been a doer, only purposing to evacuate Christ's death, and to make it of small efficacy and virtue. For whereas Christ, according as the serpent was lifted up in the wilderness, so would he himself be exalted, that thereby as many as trusted in him should have salvation; but the devil would none of that: they would have us saved by a daily oblation propitiatory, by a sacrifice expiatory, or remissory.

Now if I should preach in the country, among the unlearned, I would tell what propitiatory, expiatory, and remissory is; but here is a learned auditory: yet for them that be unlearned I will expound it. Propitiatory, expiatory, remissory, or satisfactory, for they signify all one thing in effect, and is nothing else but a thing whereby to obtain remission of sins, and to have salvation. And this way the devil used to evacuate the death of Christ, that we might have affiance in other things, as in the daily sacrifice of the priest; whereas Christ would have us to trust in his only sacrifice. So he was, *Agnus occisus ab origine mundi*; 'The Lamb that hath been slain from the beginning of the world'; and therefore he is called *juge sacrificium*, 'a continual sacrifice'; and not for the continuance of the mass, as the blanchers have blanched it, and wrested it; and as I myself did once betake it. But Paul saith, *per semetipsum purgatio facta*: 'By himself', and by none other, Christ 'made purgation' and satisfaction for the whole world.

Would Christ this word, 'by himself', had been better weighed and looked upon, and *in sanctificationem*, to make them holy; for he is *juge sacrificium*, 'a continual sacrifice', in effect, fruit and operation; that like as they, which seeing the serpent hang up in the desert, were put in remembrance of Christ's death, in whom as many as believed were saved; so all men that trusted in the death of Christ shall be saved, as well they that were before, as they that came after. For he was a continual sacrifice, as I said, in effect, fruit, operation, and virtue; as though he had from the beginning of the world, and continually should to the world's end, hang still on the cross; and he is as fresh hanging on the cross now, to them that believe and trust in him, as he was fifteen hundred years ago, when he was crucified.

Then let us trust upon his only death, and look for none other sacrifice propitiatory, than the same bloody sacrifice, the lively sacrifice; and not the dry sacrifice, but a bloody sacrifice. For Christ himself said, *consummatum est*: 'It is perfectly finished: I have taken at my Father's hand the dispensation of redeeming mankind, I have wrought man's redemption, and have despatched the matter.' Why then mingle ye him? Why do ye divide him? Why make you of him more sacrifices than one? Paul saith, *Pascha nostrum immolatus est Christus*: 'Christ our passover is offered'; so that the thing is done, and Christ hath done it, and he hath done it *semel*, once for all; and it was a bloody sacrifice, not a dry sacrifice. Why then, it is not the mass that availeth or profiteth for the quick and the dead.

Wo worth thee, O devil, wo worth thee, that hast prevailed so far and so long; that hast made England to worship false gods, forsaking Christ their Lord. Wo worth thee, devil, wo worth thee, devil, and all thy angels. If Christ by his death draweth all things to himself, and draweth all men to salvation, and to heavenly bliss, that trust in him; then the priests at the mass, at the popish mass, I say, what can they draw, when Christ draweth all, but lands and goods from the right heirs? The priests draw goods and riches, benefices and promotions to themselves; and such as believed in their sacrifices they draw to the devil. But Christ is he that draweth souls unto him by his bloody sacrifice. What have we to do then but *epulari in Domino*, to eat in the Lord at his supper? What other service have we to do to him, and what other sacrifice have we to offer, but the mortification of our flesh? What other oblation have we to make, but of obedience, of good living, of good works, and of helping our neighbours? But as for our redemption, it is done already, it cannot be better: Christ hath done that thing so well, that it cannot be amended. It cannot be devised how to make that any better than he hath done it. But the devil, by the help of that Italian bishop yonder, his chaplain, hath laboured by all means that he might to frustrate the death of Christ and the merits of his passion. And they have devised for that purpose to make us believe in other vain things by his pardons; as to have remission of sins for praying on hallowed beads; for drinking of the bakehouse bowl;[1] as a canon of Waltham Abbey once told me, that whensoever they put their loaves of bread into the oven, as many as drank of the pardon-bowl should have pardon for drinking of it. A mad thing, to give pardon to a bowl! Then to pope Alexander's[2] holy water, to hallowed bells, palms, candles, ashes, and what not? And of these things, every one hath taken away some part of Christ's sanctification; every one hath robbed some part of Christ's passion and cross, and hath mingled Christ's death, and hath been made to be propitiatory and satisfactory, and to put away sin. Yea, and Alexander's holy water yet at this day remaineth in England, and is used for a remedy against spirits and to chase away devils; yea, and I would this had been the worst. I would this were the worst. But

---

1 In the monastery of Bury St Edmunds there was a 'holye relique which was called the *pardon-boule*; whosoever dronk of this boule in the worshippe of God and Saynt Edmund, he had fiue hundred days of pardon, *toties quoties*'.
2 Pope Alexander I.

wo worth thee, O devil, that hast prevailed to evacuate Christ's cross, and to mingle the Lord's supper. These be the Italian bishop's devices, and the devil hath pricked at this mark to frustrate the cross of Christ: he shot at this mark long before Christ came, he shot at it four thousand years before Christ hanged on the cross, or suffered his passion.

For the brasen serpent was set up in the wilderness, to put men in remembrance of Christ's coming; that like as they which beheld the brasen serpent were healed of their bodily diseases, so they that looked spiritually upon Christ that was to come, in him should be saved spiritually from the devil. The serpent was set up in memory of Christ to come; but the devil found means to steal away the memory of Christ's coming, and brought the people to worship the serpent itself, and to cense him, to honour him, and to offer to him, to worship him, and to make an idol of him. And this was done by the market-men that I told you of. And the clerk of the market did it for the lucre and advantage of his master, that thereby his honour might increase; for by Christ's death he could have but small worldly advantage. And so even now so hath he certain blanchers belonging to the market, to let and stop the light of the gospel, and to hinder the king's proceedings in setting forth the word and glory of God. And when the king's majesty, with the advice of his honourable council, goeth about to promote God's word, and to set an order in matters of religion, there shall not lack blanchers that will say, 'As for images, whereas they have used to be censed, and to have candles offered unto them, none be so foolish to do it to the stock or stone, or to the image itself; but it is done to God and his honour before the image.' And though they should abuse it, these blanchers will be ready to whisper the king in the ear, and to tell him, that this abuse is but a small matter; and that the same, with all other like abuses in the church, may be reformed easily. 'It is but a little abuse,' they say, 'and it may be easily amended. But it should not be taken in hand at the first, for fear of trouble or further inconveniences. The people will not bear sudden alterations; an insurrection may be made after sudden mutation, which may be to the great harm and loss of the realm. Therefore all things shall be well, but not out of hand, for fear of further business.' These be the blanchers, that hitherto have stopped the word of God, and hindered the true setting forth of the same. There be so many put-offs, so many put-byes, so many respects and considerations of worldly wisdom: and I doubt not but there were blanchers in the old time to whisper in the ear of good king Hezekiah, for the maintenance of idolatry done to the brasen serpent, as well as there hath been now of late, and be now, that can blanch the abuse of images, and other like things. But good king Hezekiah would not be so blinded; he was like to Apollos, 'fervent in spirit'. He would give no ear to the blanchers; he was not moved with the worldly respects, with these prudent considerations, with these policies: he feared not insurrections of the people: he feared not lest his people would not bear the glory of God; but he, without any of these respects, or policies, or considerations, like a good king, for God's sake and for conscience sake, by and by plucked down the brasen serpent, and destroyed it utterly, and beat it to powder. He out of hand did cast out all images, he destroyed all idolatry, and clearly did extirpate all superstition. He would not hear these blanchers and worldly-wise men, but without delay followeth God's cause, and destroyeth all idolatry out of hand. Thus did good king Hezekiah; for he was like Apollos, fervent in spirit, and diligent to promote God's glory.

And good hope there is, that it shall be likewise here in England; for the king's majesty is so brought up in knowledge, virtue, and godliness, that it is not to be mistrusted but that we shall have all things well, and that the glory of God shall be spread abroad throughout all parts of the realm, if the prelates will diligently apply their plough, and be preachers rather than lords. But our blanchers, which will be lords, and no labourers, when they are commanded to go and resident upon their cures, and preach in their benefices, they would say, 'What? I have set a deputy there; I have a deputy that looketh well to my flock, and the which shall discharge my duty.' 'A deputy,' quoth he! I looked for that word all this while. And what a deputy must he be, trow ye? Even one like himself: he must be a canonist; that is to say, one that is brought up in the study of the pope's laws and decrees; one that will set forth papistry as well as himself will do; and one that will maintain all superstition and idolatry; and one that will nothing at all, or else very weakly, resist the devil's plough: yea, happy it is if he take no part with the devil; and where he should be an enemy to him, it is well if he take not the devil's part against Christ.

But in the mean time the prelates take their pleasures. They are lords, and no labourers: but the devil is diligent at his plough. He is no unpreaching prelate: he is no lordly loiterer from his cure, but a busy ploughman; so that among all the prelates, and among all the pack of them that have cure, the devil shall go for my money, for he still applieth his business. Therefore, ye unpreaching prelates, learn of the devil: to be diligent in doing of your office, learn of the devil: and if you will not learn of God, nor good men, for shame learn of the devil; *ad erubescentiam vestram dico*, 'I speak it for your shame'; if you will not learn of God, nor good men, to be diligent in your office, learn of the devil. Howbeit there is now very good hope that the king's majesty, being by the help of good governance of his most honourable counsellors trained and brought up in learning, and knowledge of God's word, will shortly provide a remedy, and set an order herein; which thing that it may so be, let us pray for him. Pray for him, good people; pray for him. Ye have great cause and need to pray for him.

The Fifth Sermon Preached Before Edward VI,
5 April 1549

Romans xv.4.

Quæcunque scripta sunt, ad nostram doctrinam scripta sunt.
All things that are written, they are written to be our
doctrine.

What doctrine is written for us in the parable of the judge and
the widow, I have opened it to you, most honourable audience.
Something as concerning the judge, I would wish and pray that
it might be a little better kept in memory, that in the set of justice
no more iniquity and unrighteousness might reign. Better a
little well kept, than a great deal forgotten. I would the judges
would take forth their lesson, that there might be no more
iniquity used, nor bribe-taking; for if there shall be bribing, they
know the peril of it, they know what shall follow. I would also
they should take an example of this judge, that did say, not that
that he thought himself, but our Saviour Christ puts him to say
that thing that was hid unto himself. Wherefore I would ye
should keep in memory, how unsearchable a man's heart is. I
would ye should remember the fall of the angels, and beware
thereby; the fall of the old world, and beware thereby; the fall
of Sodome and Gomora, and beware thereby; the fall of Loth's
wife, and beware thereby; the fall of the man that suffered of
late, and beware thereby.

I would not that miserable folk should forget the argument of
the wicked judge, to induce them to prayer; which argument is
this: If the judge, being a tyrant, a cruel man, a wicked man,
which did not call her to him, made her no promise, nor in
hearing nor helping of her cause, yet in the end of the matter, for
the importunity's sake, did help her; much more Almighty God,
which is a father, who beareth a fatherly affection, as the father

doth to the child, and is naturally merciful, and calleth us to him, with his promise that he will hear them that call upon him, that be in distress, and burdened with adversity. Remember this. You know where to have your remedy. You by your prayer can work great efficacy, and your prayer with tears is an instrument of great efficacy: it can bring many things to pass.

But what thing is that that maketh our prayer acceptable to God? Is it our babbling? No, no; it is not our babbling, nor our long prayer; there is another thing than it. The dignity and worthiness of our words is of no such virtue. For whosoever resorteth unto God, not in the confidence of his own merits, but in the sure trust of the deserving of our Saviour Jesus Christ, and in his passion; whosoever doth invocate the Father of heaven in the trust of Christ's merits, which offering is the most comfortable and acceptable offering to the Father; whosoever, I say, offereth up Christ, which is a perfect offering, he cannot be denied the thing he desireth, so that it be expedient for him to have it. It is not the babbling of our lips, nor dignity of our words, but the prayer of the heart is the offering that pleaseth, through the only means of his Son. For our prayer profiteth us, because we offer Christ to his Father. Whosoever resorteth to God without Christ, he resorteth in vain. Our prayer pleaseth because of Jesus Christ, whom we offer. So that it is faith, faith, faith is the matter. It is no prayer that is without faith, it is but a lip-labouring and mockery, without faith; it is but a little babbling.

I spake also of lack of faith; and upon that also I said, The end of the world is near at hand; for there is lack of faith now; also the defection is come, and swerving from the faith. Antichrist, the man of sin, the son of iniquity, is revealed; the latter day is at hand. Let us not think his coming is far off. But whensoever he cometh, he shall find iniquity enough, let him come when he will. What is now behind? We be eating and drinking as they were in Noe's time; and marrying, I think as wickedly as ever was. We be building, purchasing, planting, in the contempt of God's word. He may come shortly, when he will, for there is so much mischief, and swerving from the faith, reigning now in our days, as ever was in any age. It is a good warning to us all, to make ready against his coming.

This little rehearsal I have made of the things I spake in my last sermon. I will now for this day return to my question, and dissolve it, whether God's people may be governed by a governor that beareth the name of a king, or no? The Jews had a law, that when they should have a king, they should have him according to the election of God: he would not leave the election of a king to their own brains. There be some busy brains, wanton wits, that say, the name of a king is an odious name; and wrest this text of the scripture, where God seemeth to be angry and displeased with the Israelites for asking a king; expounding it very evil and odiously: as who would say, a king were an odious thing. I coming riding in my way, and calling to remembrance wherefore I was sent, that I must preach, and preach before the king's majesty, I thought it meet to frame my preaching according to a king. Musing of this, I remembered of myself a book that came from cardinal Pole,[1] master Pole, the king's traitor, which he sent to the king's majesty. I never remember that man, methink, but I remember him with a heavy heart: a witty man, a learned man, a man of a noble house; so in favour, that if he had tarried in the realm, and would have conformed himself to the king's proceedings, I heard say, and I believe it verily, that he had been bishop of York at this day. To be bidden by, he would have done much good in that part of the realm; for those quarters have always had great need of a learned man and a preaching prelate. A thing to be much lamented, that such a man should take such a way. I hear say, he readeth much S. Hierome's works, and is well seen in them; but I would he would follow St Hierome, where he expoundeth this place of scripture,[2] *'Exite de illa, populas meus'*: Almighty God saith, 'Get you from it, get you from Rome'; he calleth it the purple whore of Babylon. It had been more commendable to go from it, than to come to it. What his sayings be in his book,

1 *Pro Ecclesiasticæ Unitatis Defensione*: the object of it was to exalt the Papacy and priesthood above the sovereigns of the earth.
2 The reference is probably to the letter addressed by St Jerome to Algasia and to that written to Marcella, in the names of Paula and Eustochium. The Benedictine editors, however, do not consider the latter to be the composition of St Jerome.

I do not well remember; it is in the farthest end of my memory. He declareth himself in it to have a corrupt judgment. I have but a glimmering of it, yet in general I remember the scope of it. He goeth about to dissuade the king from his supremacy. In his persuasions he is very homely, very quick, and sharp with the king, as these cardinals will take well upon them. He saith,[1] that a king is an odious word, and toucheth the place how God was offended with the Israelites for calling for a king. Very lightly he seemeth to set forth the title of a king; as though he should mean: What is a king? What should a king take upon him to redress matters of religion? It pertaineth to our holy father of Rome. A king is a name and a title rather suffered of God as an evil thing, than allowed as a good thing. Calling this to remembrance, it was an occasion that I spake altogether before. Now I will answer to this. For the answer I must somewhat rip the eighth chapter of the first book of the Kings. And that I may have grace, &c.

To come to the opening of this matter, I must begin at the beginning of the chapter, that the unlearned, although I am sure here be a great many well learned, may the better come to the understanding of the matter: *Factum est cum senuisset Samuel, fecit filios suos judices populo,* 'It came to pass when Samuel was stricken in age, he made his sons judges over Israel.' Of Samuel I might fetch a process afar off, of the story of Eleana, who was his father, and who was his mother. Eleana, his father, had two wives, Anna and Phenenna, and did not put them away as men do now-a-days. There was debate between these two wives. Phenenna, in the doing of sacrifice, embraided Anna because she was barren and not fruitful. I might take here occasion to entreat of the duty between man and wife, which is a holy religion, but not religiously kept. But I will not enter into that matter at this time, Well, in process of time God made Anna fruitful through her devout prayer: she brought forth Samuel, who by the ordinance of God was made the high priest: father Samuel, a good man, a singular example, and singular pattern, a man alone, few such men as father Samuel was. To be short,

1 *Pro Ecclesiasticæ Unit. Defens.* Bk. II.

he was now come of age, he was an old man, an impotent man, not able to go from place to place to minister justice; he elected and chose two suffragans, two coadjutors, two co-helpers. I mean not hallowers of bells, nor christeners of bells; that is a popish suffraganship.[1] He made them to help him to discharge his office: he chose his two sons rather than other, because he knew them to be well brought up in virtue and learning. It was not for any carnal affection; he cared not for his renown or revenues, but he appointed them for the ease of the people, the one for to supply his place in Bethsabe, and the other in Bethlem; as we have now in England, for the wealth of the realm, we have two lords presidents.[2] Surely it is well done, and a goodly order: I would there were a third in another place. For the ease of his people, good father Samuel, and to discharge his office in places where he could not come himself, he set his two sons in office with him as his suffragans and as his coadjutors. Here I might take occasion to treat, what old and impotent bishops should do, what old preachers should do, when they come to impotency, to join with them preachers, (preachers, not bell-hallowers,) and to depart part of their living with them. They that will not for the office sake receive other, regard more the fleece than the flock. Father Samuel regarded not his revenues. Our Lord give them grace to be affected as he was, and to follow him!

Though I say that I would wish more lords presidents, I mean not, that I would have prelates lords presidents; nor that lords bishops should be lords presidents. As touching that, I said my mind and conscience the last year. And although it is said,

---

1 The stature 26 Hen. VIII c. 14, authorised every archbishop and bishop within the dominions of the sovereign of England, 'being disposed to have a suffragan', to nominate two fit persons for that office, of whom the crown was to select one for consecration.
2 One of Wales, and one of the North. King Henry VIII was desirous of establishing a lord president and council in the 'western parts' of England also, 'pretending it to be for their ease to receive justice at their own doors'; but the people opposed it, preferring to live under the direct government of the crown and the common law. Lords Lieutenants, however, seem about this time to have been introduced into counties as standing representatives of the crown.

præsunt, it is not meant that they should be lords presidents. The office of a presidentship is a civil office, and it cannot be that one man shall discharge both well.

It followeth in the text, *Non ambulaverunt filii ejus in viis ejus*, 'His sons walked not in his ways.' Here is the matter, here ye see the goodness of Samuel, how when he was not able to take the pains himself, for their own ease, he appointed them judges near unto them, as it were in the further parts of his realm, to have justice rightly ministered. But what followed? Though Samuel were good, and his children well brought up, look what the world can do! Ah, crafty world! whom shall not this world corrupt and deceive at one time or other? Samuel thought his sons should have proved well, but yet Samuel's sons walked not in their father's way. Why? What then? Is the son always bound to walk in the father's way? No, ye must not take it for a general rule. All sons are not to be blamed for not walking in their father's ways. Ezekias did not follow the steps of his father Ahaz, and was well allowed in it. Josias, the best king that ever was in Jewry, reformed his father's ways, who walked in worldly policy. In his youth he took away all idolatry, and purged his realm of it, and set a good order in all his dominions, and wrestled with idolatry. And although his father or his grandfather Manasses (it makes no matter whether) repented in the end, he had not time to reform things, he left it to his son to be done. Josias began, and made an alteration in his childhood; he turned all upside-down, he would suffer no idolatry to stand. Therefore you must not take it for a general rule, that the son must ever walk in his father's ways. Here I will renew that which I said before of the stiff-necked Jews, the rebellious people, that is their title; they never spake so rebelliously as to say they would not receive any alteration till their king came to age. Much less we Englishmen, if there be any such in England, may be ashamed. I wonder with what conscience folk can hear such things, and allow it.

This Josias made a notable alteration; and therefore take it not for a general rule, that the son shall always walk in his father's ways. Think not because he was slain in battle, that God was displeased with him: for herein God shewed his goodness to him wonderfully; who would not suffer him to see the captivity that he would bring upon the Israelites. He would not have him to have the sight, the feeling, and the beholding of his plague; he suffered him to be taken away before, and to be slain of the king of Egypt. Wherefore a just man must be glad when he is taken from misery: *Justus si morete præoccupatus fuerit in refrigerio erit*; 'If a just man be prevented with death, it shall be to his relief': he must think that he is one of those whom the world is not worthy to have. It came of a singular goodness of God, that he was by death delivered from the sight of that captivity. Therefore take it not for a general rule, that the son be always bound to walk in the father's ways: *Nolite in præceptis patrum vestrorum incedere*, 'Walk not in the commandments of your fathers'; for so it is said in another place of scripture. It is spoken to the reproach of Samuel's sons, that they walked not in his way, for he was a good man: a wonderful thing that these children, being so well brought up, should so fall and be corrupt. If the devil can prevail and hath power against them that had so godly education, what vantage hath he at them that be brought up in iniquity and covetousness? It is a proverb that *Magistratus virum commonstrat*, 'Office and authority sheweth what a man is.' A man knoweth not himself till he be tried. Many there be that being without office can rebuke magistrates, and find fault with men that be in office and pre-eminence: after, when it cometh to their chance to come to office themselves, then they have taken out a new lesson; *Cum essem parvulus sapiebam ut parvulus*, 'When I was a child I savoured as a child.' They will do then as other men do; they are come to have experience, to be practitioners. The maid's child is ever best taught: for he that standeth upright in office, he is the fellow. Samuel would never have thought that his sons should have been so corrupted. It is a perilous thing, a dangerous state to be a judge. They felt the smack of this world, a perilous thing: and therefore Chrysostom saith, *Miror si aliquis rectorum salvabitur*; 'I marvel,' saith he, 'that any ruler can be saved.' If the peril were well considered, men would not be so desirous as they be. The world, the world hath many subtle sleights: it is a crafty thing, and very deceitful, a corrupter; and who is it whom the world doth not corrupt and blind at one time or other? What was the way they walked? *Declinaverunt post avaritiam*, that is one: they stooped after gains, turned aside after lucre. What followed? *Acceperunt numera*, they took rewards, gifts; bribes I should call them, for that is their right name. *Perverterunt judicium*, they turned justice upside down. Either they would give wrong judgment, or else put off and delay poor men's matters. These were their ways, here is the devil's genealogy; a gradation of the devil's making: this is *scala inferni*, the ladder of hell.

I told you before of *scala cœli*, the ladder of heaven; I would you should not forget it. The steps thereof are set forth in the tenth to the Romans. The first is preaching, then hearing, then believing, and last of all salvation. *Scala cœli* is a preaching matter, I tell you, and not a massing matter. God's instrument of salvation is preaching. Here I move you, my lords, not to be greedy and outrageous in enhancing and raising of your rents to the minishing of the office of salvation. It would pity a man's heart to hear that that I hear of the state of Cambridge;[1] what it is in Oxford, I cannot tell. There be few do study divinity, but so many as of necessity must furnish the colleges; for their livings be so small, and victuals so dear, that they tarry not there, but go other where to seek livings; and so they go about. Now there be a few gentlemen, and they study a little divinity. Alas! what is that? It will come to pass that we shall have nothing but a little English divinity, that will bring the realm into a very barbarousness and utter decay of learning. It is not that, I wis, that will keep out the supremacy of the bishop of Rome.

Here I will make a supplication, that ye would bestow so much to the finding of scholars of good wits, of poor men's sons, to exercise the office of salvation, in relieving of scholars, as ye were wont to bestow in pilgrimage-matters, in trentals, in

1 About this time Roger Ascham, writing to Archbishop Cranmer, observed, 'That the university [of Cambridge] was then in so depressed and drooping a condition, that very few had hope of coming hither at all, and fewer had any comfort to make long tarrying when they were; and that abroad it retained not so much as a shadow of its ancient dignity.'

masses, in pardons, in purgatory-matters. Ye bestowed that liberally, bountifully; but this was not well spent. You had a zeal, but not *secundum scientiam*, 'not according to knowledge.' You may be sure, if you bestow your goods on this wise, ye shall bestow it well, to support and uphold God's word, wherein ye shall please God. I require no more but that ye bestow so much godly as ye were wont to bestow ungodly. It is a reasonable petition; for God's sake look upon it. I say no more. There be none now but great men's sons in colleges, and their fathers look not to have them preachers;[1] so every way this office of preaching is pinched at. I will speak no more of *scala cœli*. But I am sure this is *scala inferni*, the right way to hell, to be covetous, to take bribes, and pervert justice. If a judge should ask me the way to hell, I would shew him this way: first, let him be a covetous man, let his heart be poisoned with covetousness; then let him go a little further and take bribes; and last, pervert judgment. Lo, here is the mother and the daughter, and the daughter's daughter. Avarice is the mother, she brings forth bribe-taking, and bribe-taking perverting of judgment. There lacks a fourth thing to make up the mess, which, (so God help me!) if I were judge, should be *hangum tutum*, a Tyburn tippet to take with him, and it were the judge of the king's bench, my lord chief judge of England; yea, and it were my lord chancellor himself, to Tyburn with him. There was within these thirty years a certain widow, which suddenly was attached, had to prison, indicted, condemned, and there were certain learned men that visited her in prison. Oh, I would ye would resort to prisons! A commendable thing in a christian realm: I would wish there were curates for prisons, that we might say, the curate of Newgate, the curate of the Fleet, and I would have them waged for their labour. It is a holiday work to visit the prisoners, for they be kept from sermons. There was that resorted to this woman, who when she came to prison, was all

1 Ascham also mentions, as one of the two 'hinderances to the flourishing estate of the university,' that 'such as were admitted were for the most part only the sons of rich men, and such as never intended to pursue their studies to that degree as to arrive at any eminent proficiency and perfection in learning'.

on her beads, and nothing else, a popish woman, and savoured not of Jesu Christ. In process she was so applied, that she tasted *quam suavis est Dominus*; she had such a savour, such a sweetness and feeling, that she thought it long to the day of execution. She was with Christ already, as touching faith; she had such a desire that she said with St Paul, *Cupio dissolvi et esse cum Christo*, 'I desire to be rid, and to be with Christ.' The word of God had so wrought in her. When she was brought to punishment, she desired to confess her fault: she took of her death, that she was guiltless in that thing she suffered for, and her neighbours would have borne her witness in the same. She was always an honest civil woman; her neighbours would have gone on her purgation a great way. They would needs have her confess. 'Then,' saith she, 'I am not guilty. Would ye have me make me guilty where I am not?' Yet for all this she was a trespasser, she had done a great offence. But before I go forward with this, I must first tell you a tale. I heard a good while ago a tale of one (I saw the man that told me the tale not long ago) in this auditory. He hath travelled in more countries than one. He told me that there was once a prætor in Rome, lord mayor of Rome, a rich man, one of the richest merchants in all the city, and suddenly he was cast in the castle Angel.[1] It was heard of, and ever man whispered in another's ear, 'What hath he done? Hath he killed any man?' 'No.' 'Hath he meddled with alum, our holy father's merchandise?'[2] 'No.' 'Hath he counterfeited our holy father's bulls?' 'No.' For these were high treasons. One rounded another in the ear, and said, *Erat dives*, 'He was a rich man': a great fault. Here was a goodly prey for that holy father.

1 Castle of St Angelo.
2 In Europe, the art of boiling alum seems to have been first known in Italy. Several factories for that substance were soon established in various parts of that country; but Pope Pius II never rested until he had obtained all the alum factories and the whole trade transferred into his own hands. He then endeavoured, by every possible means, to prevent foreigners from acquiring any knowledge of the art of boiling alum; and prohibited free-trade in that article as a sin, and under the terror of excommunication. Later popes maintained the monopoly by the same spiritual powers.

It was in pope Julius's[1] time; he was a great warrior. This prey would help him to maintain his wars; a jolly prey for our holy father. So this woman was *dives*: she was a rich woman, she had her lands by the sheriff's nose. He was a gentleman of a long nose. Such a cup, such a cover! She would not depart from her own. This sheriff was a covetous man, a worldly man. The judge, at the impanelling of the quest, had his grave looks, and charged them with this: 'It was the king's matter, look well upon it.' When it makes for their purpose, they have 'The King, the King', in their mouths. Well, somewhat there was, there was the walking of angels[2] between them. I would wish that of such a judge in England now we might have the skin hanged up. It were a goodly sign, the sign of the judge's skin. It should be Lot's wife to all judges that should follow after.

[3 By this ye may perceive it is possible for a man to answer for himself, and be arraigned at the bar, and nevertheless to have wrong: yea, ye shall have it in form of law, and yet have wrong too. So it is possible, in a case, for a man that hath in his absence attaintment, to have right and no wrong. I will not say nay but it is a good law for a man to answer for himself: this is reasonable, allowable, and good. And yet such an urgent cause may be, such a respect to a commonwealth, that a man may rightly be condemned in his absence. There be such causes that a man may in his absence be condemned, but not oft, except they be such cases that the reason of general law may be kept. I am provoked of some to condemn this law, but I am not able, so it be but for a time, and upon weighty considerations; so that it be used rarely, seldomly: for avoiding disturbance in the

1 Julius II whose whole pontificate was spent amid violence and bloodshed.
2 A gold coin so called, which bore on one side of it the figure of the archangel Michael and the dragon.
3 The passage in brackets is inserted frm the editions of 1549 and 1562. It is an attempt to vindicate the parliament which passed the act (2 and 3 Edward VI c. 18,) for attainting the lord admiral, without allowing him to be present, to object to the evidence brought against him or to be heard in his defence.

commonwealth, such an epiky[1] and moderation may be used in it. And nevertheless it is very meet and requisite that a man should answer for himself. We must consider the ground of the law: for *Ratio legis anima legis*, 'The reason of the law is the soul of the law.' Why? What is the reason and end of the law? It is this, that no man should be injured. A man may in his attaintment have no more wrong done him than if he answered for himself. Ah! then I am not able to say, that in no wise an arraignment may be turned into attaintment. A man may have wrong, and that in open judgment and in form of law, and yet allowed to answer for himself; and even so is possible he may have right, though he never answer for himself. I will not say but that the parliament-houses, both high and low, may err, and yet they may do well, and christian subjects must take all things to the best, and expound their doings well, although they cannot yield a reason for it, except their proceedings be manifestly wicked. For though they cannot attain to see for what purpose things be done, it is no good reason that they be called evil done therefore. And is this a good argument, 'He is not allowed to answer for himself in this place or that place, where he will appoint, *ergo*, he is not allowed to answer for himself?' No: he might have answered the best he could for himself before a great many, and have had more too if he had required them: yea, and was commanded upon his allegiance to speak for himself and to make answer; but he would not. Needs he would come out to judgment, and appoint the place himself. A man that answers for himself at the bar is not allowed his man of law to answer for him, but he must answer himself. Yet in the parliament, although he were not there himself, any friend he had had liberty to answer for him, frank and free. I know of the old manner: the tenor of the writs is this, – every man to speak the best he knoweth of his conscience, for the king's majesty's honour, and the wealth of the realm. There were in the parliament, in both houses, a great many learned

---

1 (ἐπιείκεια) is that parte of justice called in Latine *æquum* and *bonum*: in English there is not any one word to express the meaning, which basically refers to causing the least detriment.

men, conscionable men, wise men. When that man was attainted there, and they had liberty there to say nay to his attaintment if they would; sure I am they most allowed it, or else it could not have gone forward.

These premises considered, I would have you to bear such a heart as it becometh christian subjects. I know what men say of me well enough. I could purge myself. There is that provokes me to speak against this law of attaintment: they say I am not indifferent. Surely I would have it to be done rarely, upon some great respect to the commonwealth, for avoiding of greater tumult and peril. St Paul was allowed to answer for himself: if Lysias the tribune had not plucked him away from shewing of his matter, it had cost him his life. Where he was saved by the magistrate, being but a private man; will ye not allow that something be done as well for saving of the magistrate's life? It behoves them of the parliament to look well upon the matter: and I, for my part, think not but they did well; else I should not yield the duty of a subject. Some liken me to doctor Shaw, that preached at Paul's Cross, that king Edward's sons were bastards.[1] An easy matter for one of the council to do as doctor Shaw did. Methink you, being the king's servant and his officer, should think better on the king and his council, though I were light of belief. If he had been a true man to his master, he would never have spoken it. The council needs not my lie for the defence of that that they do. I can bear it of myself. Concerning myself, that which I have spoken hath done some good. You will say this: the parliament-house are wiser than I am, you might leave them to the defence of themselves. Although the men of the parliament-house can defend themselves, yet have I spoken this of a good zeal, and a good ground, of the admiral's writing; I have not feigned nor lied one jot, I take God to witness. Use therefore your judgment and languages as it becometh christian subjects. I will now leave the honourable council to answer for themselves. He confessed one fact, he would have

1 The object of Shaw's preaching was to invalidate the title of the sons of Edward IV to the crown, and so to support the claims of Richard III.

had the governance of the king's majesty. And wot you why? He said he would not, in his minority, have him brought up like a ward. I am sure he hath been brought up so godly, with such schoolmasters, as never king was in England, and so hath prospered under them as never none did. I wot not what he meant by his bringing up like a ward, unless he would have him not to go to his book and learn as he doth. Now wo worth him! Yet I will not say so neither, but I pray God amend him, or else God send him short life, that would have my sovereign not to be brought up in learning, and would pluck him from his book. I advertise thee therefore, my fellow-subject, use thy tongue better, and expound well the doings of the magistrates.

Now to the purpose; for these things let me of my matter. Some say preachers should not meddle with such matters; but did not our Saviour Jesus Christ meddle with matters of judgment, when he spake of the wicked judge, to leave example to us to follow, to do the same?] Ye see here that lady Covetousness is a fruitful woman, ever childing, and ever bringing forth her fruits. It is a true saying, *Radix omnium malorum avaritia*, 'Covetousness is the root of all wickedness.' One will say, peradventure, 'You speak unseemly and inconveniently, so to be against the officers for taking rewards in doing pleasures. Ye consider not the matter to the bottom. Their offices be bought for great sums; now how should they receive their money again but by bribing? Ye would have them undone. Some of them gave two hundred pound, some five hundred pound, some two thousand pound: and how shall they gather up this money again, but by helping themselves in their office?' And is it so, trow ye? Are civil offices bought for money? Lord God, who would have thought that! Let us not be too hasty to credit it: for then we have the old proverb, *Omnia venalia Romæ*, 'All things are sold for money at Rome'; and Rome is come home to our own doors. If they buy, they must needs sell; for it is wittily spoken,[1] *Vendere jure potest, emerat ille prius*, 'He may lawfully sell it, he bought it before.' God forfend that ever any

1 Of Pope Alexander VI.

such enormity should be in England, that civil offices should be bought and sold; whereas men should have them given them for their worthiness! I would the king's majesty should seek through his realm for meet men, and able men, worthy to be in office, yea, and give them liberally for their pains; and rather give them money to take the office in hand, than they to give money for it. This buying of offices is a making of bribery; it is an inducing and enforcing and compelling of men to bribery. Holy scripture qualifieth the officers, and sheweth what manner of men they should be, and of what qualities, *viros fortes*, some translations have, *viros sapientes*, 'wise men'; the English translation hath it very well, 'men of activity', that have stomachs to do their office: they must not be milksops, nor white-livered knights; they must be wise, hearty, hardy, men of a good stomach. Secondarily, he qualifieth them with the fear of God: he saith they must be *timentes Deum*, 'fearing God'. For if he fear God, he shall be no briber, no perverter of judgment, faithful. Thirdly, they must be chosen officers, in *quibus est veritas*, 'in whom is truth'; if he say it, it shall be done. Fourthly, *qui oderunt avaritiam*, 'hating covetousness'; far from it; he will not come near it that hateth it. It is not he that will give five hundred pound for an office. With these qualities God's wisdom would have magistrates to be qualified.

This cometh from the devil's consistory, to pay five hundred pound for one office. If they pay so much, it must needs follow that they take bribes, that they be bribe-takers. Such as be meet to bear office, seek them out, hire them, give them competent and liberal fees, that they shall not need to take any bribes. And if ye be a selling civil offices, ye are as they which sell their benefices; and so we shall have *omnia venalia*, all things bought for money. I marvel the ground gapes not and devours us: howbeit, we ought not to marvel; surely it is the great lenity of God that suffers it. O Lord, in what case are we! If the great men in Turkey should use in their religion of Mahomet to sell, as our patrons commonly sell benefices here, the office of preaching, the office of salvation, it should be taken as an intolerable thing; the Turk would not suffer it in his commonwealth. Patrons be charged to see the office done, and not to seek a lucre and a gain by their patronship. There was a patron in England, when it was that he had a benefice fallen into his hand, and a good brother of mine came unto him, and brought him thirty apples in a dish, and gave them his man to carry them to his master. It is like he gave one to his man for his labour, to make up the game, and so there was thirty-one. This man cometh to his master, and presented him with the dish of apples, saying, 'Sir such a man hath sent you a dish of fruit, and desireth you to be good unto him for such a benefice.' 'Tush, tush,' quoth he, 'this is no apple matter; I will have none of his apples; I have as good as these, or as he hath any, in mine own orchard.' The man came to the priest again, and told him what his master said. 'Then,' quoth the priest, 'desire him yet to prove one of them for my sake; he shall find them much better than they look for.' He cut one of them, and found ten pieces of gold in it. 'Marry,' quoth he, 'this is a good apple.' The priest standing not far off, hearing what the gentleman said, cried out and answered, 'They are all one apple, I warrant you, sir; they grew all on one tree, and have all one taste.' 'Well, he is a good fellow, let him have it,' quoth the patron. Get you a graft of this tree, and I warrant you it will stand you in better stead than all St Paul's learning. Well, let patrons take heed; for they shall answer for all the souls that perish through their default. There is a saying, that there be a great many in England that say there is no soul, that believe not in the immortality of man's soul, that think it is not eternal, but like a dog's soul, that think there is neither heaven or hell. O Lord, what a weighty matter is this! What a lamentable thing in a christian commonwealth! I cannot tell what they say; but I perceive by these works that they think so, or else they would never do as they do. These sellers of offices shew that they believe that there is neither hell nor heaven: it is taken for a laughing matter.

Well, I will go on. Now to the chapter. The children of Israel came to Samuel, and said, *Senuisti*; 'Thou art grown into age, give us a king; thy sons walk not in thy ways.' What a heaviness was this to father Samuel's heart, to hear that his sons, whom he had so well brought up, should swerve from his ways that he had walked in! Father Samuel goeth to God, to know his will and pleasure in this matter. God answered, 'Let them have a king; they have not cast thee away, but me, that I should not reign over them.' This is their ground, that say a king is an odious thing, and not acceptable before the face of God. Thus they force and violate this place, to make it for their purpose; where no such thing is meant. 'Shew the Israelites,' saith God, 'and testify to them a king's authority, and what a king is, and what a king will do. If that will not persuade them, I will not hear them hereafter when they shall cry unto me.'

I must needs confess that the Jews trespassed against God in asking a king; but here is the matter, in what thing their offence stood, whether absolutely in asking a king, or in any other circumstance. It was in a circumstance: they said not, Ask us a king of God; but, Make us a king to judge us, as all other nations have. They would have a king of their own swing, and of their own election, as though they passed not of God. In another point there was pride; they would be like the heathen, and judged under kings, as they were. Thirdly, they offended God, because they asked a king to the injury and wrong of good father Samuel, to depose him; so this was a wrong toward Samuel. It was not with Samuel and his children, Idel and Abia, like as with Eli and his children, Ophnia and Phinees. They were cruel, who with hooks taking the flesh out of the pots, when that sacrifice was offered to God, brought the people into a contempt of God's word. They were lecherers; their sin was manifestly and notoriously known: but their father Eli, knowing and hearing of it, did blame them, but nothing to the purpose; he did not earnestly and substantially chastise them, and therefore he was justly deposed of God. The sins of Samuel's sons were not known; they were not so notorious: wherefore it was not with father Samuel as it was with Eli; his sons' faults were taking of bribes, and perverting of judgments. Ye know that bribery is a secret fault, and therefore it was not known: it was done under a colour and a pretence of justice, hiddenly and covertly done: therefore because it stood in bribes, it was not like in Samuel as in Eli. It is a dangerous thing to be in office; for *qui attingit picem coinquinabitur ab ea*; 'He that meddleth with pitch is like to be spotted with it.' Bribes may be assembled[1] to pitch; for even as pitch doth pollute their hands that meddle with it, so bribes will bring you to perverting of justice. Beware of pitch, you judges of the world; bribes will make you pervert justice. 'Why,' you will say, 'we touch none.' No, marry, but my mistress your wife hath a fine finger, she toucheth it for you: or else you have a servant, a *mune-ribus*; he will say, 'if you will come to my master and offer him a yoke of oxen, you shall speed never the worse; but I think my master will take none.' When he hath offered them to the master, then comes another servant and says, 'If you will bring them to the clerk of the kitchen, you shall be remembered the better.' This is a friarly fashion, that will receive no money in their hands, but will have it put upon their sleevers; a goodly rag of popish religion. They be like Gray Friars, that will not be seen to receive bribes themselves, but have others to receive for them.[2]

Though Samuel's sons were privy bribers, and kept the thing very close, yet the cry of the people brought it to Samuel. It was a hid kind of sin: for men in this point would face it, and brazen it, and make a shew of upright dealing, when they be most guilty. Nevertheless, this gear came out. O wicked sons, that brought both their father to deposition, and themselves to shame! When Samuel heard of their fault, he went not about to excuse their faults: he would not *communicare peccatis alienis*, be partaker with his sons' offences: he said, *Ego senui, ecce filii mei vobiscum sunt*. As soon as he heard of it, he delivered his sons to the people to be punished. He went not about to excuse them, nor said not, 'This is the first time, bear with them'; but presented them by and by to the people, saying 'Lo, here they be, take them, do with them according to their deserts.' Oh, I would there were no more bearers of other men's sins than this good father Samuel was!

I heard of late of a notable bloodshed: '*Audio*,' saith St Paul; and so do I: I know it not, but I hear of it. There was a searcher in London which, executing his office, displeased a

---

1 Assembled: i.e. assimilated, likened.
2 The Franciscan or Grey friars rule forbade its members to seek monetary reward either by themselves or through a third party.

merchantman, insomuch that when he was doing his office there were at words: the merchantman threatened him; the searcher said the king should not lose his custom. The merchant goes me home, and sharpens his wood-knife, and comes again and knocks him on the head, and kills him. They that told me the tale say it is winked at; they look through their fingers, and will not see it. Whether it be taken up with a pardon, or no, I cannot tell; but this I am sure, and if ye bear with such matters, the devil shall bear you away to hell. Bloodshed and murder would have no bearing. It is a heinous thing bloodshedding, and especially voluntary murder and prepensed murder. For in Numbers God saith, it polluteth the whole realm: *Polluitur illa terra*, &c., *et non potest expiari sine sanguine*; 'The land cannot be purified nor cleansed again, till his blood be shed that shed it.' It is the office of a king to see such murderers punished with death; for *non frustra gestat gladium*. What will you make of a king? He beareth a sword before him, not a peacock's feather. I go not about to stir you now to cruelty; but I speak against the bearing of bloodshed: this bearing must be looked upon. In certain causes of murder such great circumstances may be, that the king may pardon a murder. But if I were worthy to be of counsel, or if I were asked mine advice, I would not have the king to pardon a voluntary murder, a prepensed murder.

I can tell where one man slew another in a township, and was attached upon the same: twelve men were impanelled: the man had friends: the sheriff laboured the bench: the twelve men stuck at it, and said, 'Except he would disburse twelve crowns, they would find him guilty.' Means were found that the twelve crowns were paid. The quest comes in, and says 'Not guilty.' Here was 'not guilty' for twelve crowns. This is a bearing, and if some of the bench were hanged, they were well served. This makes men bold to do murder and slaughter. We should reserve murdering till we come to our enemies, and the king bid us fight: he that would bestir him then were a pretty fellow indeed. Crowns! if their crowns were shaven to the shoulders, they were served well enough.

I know where a woman was got with child, and was ashamed at the matter, and went into a secret place, where she had no woman at her travail, and was delivered of three children at a birth. She wrung their necks, and cast them into a water, and so killed her children: suddenly she was gaunt[1] again; and her neighbours suspecting the matter, caused her to be examined, and she granted all. Afterward she was arraigned at the bar for it, and despatched and found not guilty, through bearing of friends, and bribing of the judge: where, at the same sessions, another poor woman was hanged for stealing a few rags off a hedge that were not worth a crown.

There was a certain gentleman, a professor of the word of God, (he sped never the better for that, ye may be sure,) who was accused for murdering of a man, whereupon he was cast into prison; and by chance, as he was in prison, one of his friends came unto him for to visit him; and he declared to his friend that he was never guilty in the murdering of the man: so he went his ways. The gentleman was arraigned and condemned; and as he went to his execution, he saw his friend's servant, and said unto him, 'Commend me to thy master, and I pray thee tell him, I am the same man still I was when he was with me; and if thou tarry awhile, thou shalt see me die.' There was suit made for this man's pardon, but it could not be gotten. Belike the sheriffs or some other bare him no good will: but he died for it. And afterward, I being in the Tower, having leave to come to the lieutenant's table, I heard him say, that there was a man hanged afterward that killed the same man for whom this gentleman was put to death. O Lord, what bearing, what bolstering of naughty matters is this in a christian realm! I desire your Majesty to remedy the matter, and God grant you to see redress in this realm in your own person. Although my lord Protector, I doubt not, and the rest of the council do, in the mean while, all that lieth in them to redress things; I would such as be rulers, noblemen, and masters, should be at this point with their servants, to certify them on this sort: If any man go about to do you wrong, I will do my best to help you in your right; but if ye break the law, ye shall have justice. If ye will be man-quellers, murderers, and transgressors, look for no bearing at my hands.

1 Thin, slender.

A strange thing! What need we in the vengeance to burden ourselves with other men's sins? Have we not sins enow of our own? What need have I to burden myself with other men's sins? I have burdens and two heaps of sins, one heap of known sins, another of unknown sins. I had need to say, *Ab occultis meis munda me, Domine*; 'O Lord, deliver me from my hidden and my unknown sins.' Then if I bear with other men's sins, I must say: Deliver me from my other men's sins. A strange saying: from my other men's sins! Who beareth with other folks' offences, he communicateth with other folks' sins. Men have sins enough of their own, although they bear not and bolster up other men in their naughtiness. This bearing, this bolstering, and looking through their fingers, is naught. What the fair hap should I, or any else, increase my burden? My other men's sins forgive me, O Lord: a strange language! they have hid sins of their own enough, although they bear not with guiltiness of other men's sins.

Oh, father Samuel would not bear his own sons; he offered his own sons to punishment, and said, *Ecce filii mei vobiscum sunt*: even at the first time he said, 'Lo, here they be: I discharge myself; take them unto you: as for my part, *Præsto sum loqui coram Domino et Christo ejus*: I am here ready to answer for myself before the Lord, and his anointed. Behold, here I am, record of me before the Lord, *utrum cujusquam bovem*, &c., whether I have taken any man's ox, any man's ass, or whether I have done any man wrong, or hurt any man, or taken any bribes at any man's hand.' I can commend the English translation, that doth interpret *munera*, bribes, not gifts. They answered, 'Nay, forsooth, we know no such things in you.' *Testis est mihi Deus*, saith he, 'God is witness,' *quod nihil inveneritis in manu mea*, 'That you have found nought in my hands.' Few such Samuels are in England, nor in the world. Why did Samuel this? Marry, to purge himself; he was enforced to it, for he was wrongly deposed.

Then by this ye may perceive the fault of the Jews, for they offended not God in asking of a king, but in asking for a king to the wronging and deposition of good father Samuel. If after Samuel's death the people had asked of God a king, they had not faulted: but it is no small fault to put an innocent out of his office. King David likewise commanded his people to be numbered, and therewith offended God grievously. Why, might he not know the number of his people? Yes, it was not the numbering of the people that offended God, for a king may number his people; but he did it of a pride, of an elation of mind, not according to God's ordinance, but as having a trust in the number of his men: this offended God. Likewise the Jews asked a king, and therewith they offended not God; but they asked him with such circumstances, that God was offended with them. It is no small fault to put a just man out of his office, and to depose him unworthily. To choose a king contrarying the ordinance of God, is a casting away of God, and not of a king. Therefore doubt not but the title of a king is a lawful thing, is a lawful title, as of other magistrates. Only let the kings take heed that they do as it becometh kings to do, that they do their office well. It is a great thing, a chargeable thing. Let them beware that they do not *communicare peccatis alienis*, that they bear not with other men's faults; for they shall give a strait account for all that perisheth through their negligence. We perceive now what this text meaneth. It is written in the last of Judges, *In diebus illis non erat rex in Israel*: 'In those days there was no king in Israel; every man did that which seemed right in his own eyes.' Men were then allowed to do what they would. When men may be allowed to do what they will, then it is as good to have no king at all. Here is a wonderful matter, that unpreaching prelates should be suffered so long. They can allege for themselves seven hundred years. This while the realm had been as good to have no king. Likewise these bribing judges have been suffered of a long time: and then it was *quasi non fuisset rex in Anglia*. To suffer this is as much as to say, 'There is no king in England.' It is the duty of a king to have all states set in order to do their office.

I have troubled you too long. I will make an end. 'Blessed be they that hear the word of God,' but so that they follow it, and keep it in credit, in memory, not to deprave it and slander it, and bring the preachers out of credit, but that follow it in their life and live after it. He grant you all that blessing, that made both you and me! *Amen*.

The Seventh Sermon Preached Before Edward VI, 19 April 1549

Romans xv.4.

Quæcunque scripta sunt, ad nostram doctrinam scripta sunt.
All things that be written, they be written to be our doctrine.

By occasion of this text, most honourable audience, I have walked this Lent in the broad field of scripture, and used my liberty, and entreated of such matters as I thought meet for this auditory. I have had ado with many estates, even with the highest of all. I have entreated of the duty of kings, of the duty of magistrates and judges, of the duty of prelates; allowing that that is good, and disallowing the contrary. I have taught that we are all sinners: I think there is none of us all, neither preacher nor hearer, but we may be amended, and redress our lives: we may all say, yea, all the pack of us, *Peccavimus cum patribus nostris*, 'We have offended and sinned with our forefathers.' *In multis offendimus omnes*: there is none of us all but we have in sundry things grievously offended almighty God. I here entreated of many faults, and rebuked many kinds of sins. I intend to-day, by God's grace, to shew you the remedy of sin. We be in the place of repentance: now is the time to call for mercy, whilst we be in this world. We be all sinners, even the best of us all; therefore it is good to hear the remedy of sin. This day is commonly called Good-Friday: although every day ought to be with us Good-Friday, yet this day we are accustomed specially to have a commemoration and remembrance of the passion of our Saviour Jesus Christ. This day we have in memory his bitter passion and death, which is the remedy of our sin. Therefore I intend to entreat of a piece of a story of his passion; I am not able to entreat of all. That I may do that the better, and that it may be to the honour of God, and the edification of your souls, and mine both, I shall desire you to pray. In this prayer I will desire you to remember the souls departed, with lauds and praise to almighty God, and that he did vouchsafe to assist them at the hour of their death: in so doing you shall be put in remembrance to pray for yourselves, that it may please God to assist and comfort you in the agonies and pains of death.

The place that I will entreat of is the twenty-sixth chapter of St Matthew. Howbeit, as I entreat of it, I will borrow part of St Mark, and part of St Luke: for they have somewhat that St Matthew hath not; and especially Luke. The text is, *Tunc cum venisset Jesus in villam, quæ dicitur Gethsemani*, 'Then when Jesus came'; some have *in villam*, some *in agrum*, some *in prædium*. But it is all one; when Christ came into a grange, into a piece of land, into a field, it makes no matter; call it what ye will. At what time he had come into an honest man's house, and there eaten his paschal lamb, and instituted and celebrated the Lord's supper, and set forth the blessed communion; then when this was done, he took his way to the place where he knew Judas would come. It was a solitary place, and thither he went with his eleven apostles: for Judas, the twelfth, was about his business, he was occupied about his merchandise, and was providing among the bishops and priests to come with an ambushment of Jews, to take our Saviour Jesu Christ. And when he came into the field or grange, this village, or farm-place, which was called Gethsemane, there was a garden, saith Luke, into the which he goeth, and leaves eight of his disciples without; howbeit he appointed them what they should do: he saith, *Sedete hic donec illuc vadam et orem*; 'Sit you here, whilst I go yonder and pray.' He told them that he went to pray, to monish them what they should do, to fall to prayer as he did. He left them there, and took no more with him but three, Peter, James, and John, to teach us that a solitary place is meet for prayer. Then when he was come into this garden *cœpit expavascere*, 'he began to tremble', insomuch he said, *Tristis est anima mea usque ad mortem*, 'My soul is heavy and pensive even unto death.'

74

This is a notable place, and one of the most especial and chiefest of all that be in the story of the passion of Christ. Here is our remedy: here we must have in consideration all his doings and sayings, for our learning, for our edification, for our comfort and consolation.

First of all, he set his three disciples that he took with him in order, and told them what they should do, saying *Sedet hic, et vigilate mecum, et orate*; 'Sit here, and pray that ye enter not into temptation.' But of that I will entreat afterward. Now when he was in the garden, *Cœpit expavescere*, he began to be heavy, pensive, heavy-hearted. I like not Origen's playing with this word *cœpit*: it was a perfect heaviness; it was such a one as was never seen a greater; it was not only the beginning of a sorrow. These doctors, we have great cause to thank God for them, but yet I would not have them always to be allowed. They have handled many points of our faith very godly; and we may have a great stay in them in many things; we might not well lack them: but yet I would not have men to be sworn to them, and so addict, as to take hand over head whatsoever they say: it were a great inconvenience so to do.

Well, let us go forward. He took Peter, James, and John, into this garden. And why did he take them with him, rather than other? Marry, those that he had taken before, to whom he had revealed in the hill the transfiguration and declaration of his deity, to see the revelation of the majesty of his Godhead, now in the garden he revealed to the same the infirmity of his manhood: because they had tasted of the sweet, he would they should taste also of the sour. He took these with him at both times: for two or three is enough to bear witness. And he began to be heavy in his mind; he was greatly vexed within himself, he was sore afflicted, it was a great heaviness. He had been heavy many times before; and he had suffered great afflictions in his soul, as for the blindness of the Jews; and he was like to suffer more pangs of pain in his body. But this pang was greater than any that he ever suffered: yea, it was a greater torment unto him, I think a greater pain, than when he was hanged on the cross; than when the four nails were knocked and driven through his hands and feet; than when the sharp crown of thorns was thrust on his head. This was the heaviness and pensiveness of his heart, the agony of the spirit. And as the soul is more precious than the body, even so is the pain of the soul more grievous than the pains of the body: therefore there is another which writeth, *Horror mortis gravior ipsa morte*; 'The horror and ugsomeness of death is sorer than death itself.'[1] This is the most grievous pain that ever Christ suffered, even this pang that he suffered in the garden. It is the most notable place, one of them in the whole story of the passion, when he said, *Anima mea tristis est usque ad mortem*, 'My soul is heavy to death'; and *cum cœpisset expavescere*, 'when he began to quiver, to shake.' The grievousness of it is declared by this prayer that he made: *Pater, si possibile est*, &c., 'Father , if it be possible, away with this cup: rid me of it.' He understood by this cup his pains of death; for he knew well enough that his passion was at hand, that Judas was coming upon him with the Jews to take him.

There was offered unto him now the image of death; the image, the sense, the feeling of hell: for death and hell go both together. I will entreat of this image of hell, which is death. Truly no man can shew it perfectly, yet I will do the best I can to make you understand the grievous pangs that our Saviour Christ was in when he was in the garden. As man's power is not able to bear it, so no man's tongue is able to express it. Painters paint death like a man without skin, and a body having nothing but bones. And hell they paint with horrible flames of burning fire: they bungle somewhat at it, they come nothing near it. But this is no true painting. No painter can paint hell, unless he could paint the torment and condemnation both of body and soul; the possession and having of all infelicity. This is hell, this is the image of death: this is hell, such an evil-favoured face, such an uglesome countenance, such an horrible visage our Saviour Christ saw of death and hell in the garden. There is no pleasure in beholding of it, but more pain than any tongue can tell. Death and hell took unto them this evil-favoured face of sin, and through sin. This sin is so highly hated

1 Erasmus, in his paraphrase on this passage, *Est autem mortis horror, si quando corripuit hominem, vel ipsa morte acerbior.*

76

of God, that he doth pronounce it worthy to be punished with lack of all felicity, with the feeling of infelicity. Death and hell be not only the wages, the reward, the stipend of sin: but they are brought into the world by sin. *Per peccatum mors*, saith St Paul, 'through sin death entered into the world.' Moses sheweth the first coming in of it into the world. Whereas our first father Adam was set at liberty to live for ever, yet God inhibiting him from eating of the apple, told him: 'If thou meddle with this fruit, thou and all thy posterity shall fall into necessity of death, from ever living: *morte morieris*, thou and all thy posterity shall be subject to death.' Here came in death and hell: sin was their mother; therefore they must have such an image as their mother sin would give them.

An uglesome thing and an horrible image must it needs be, that is brought in by such a thing so hated of God; yea, this face of death and hell is so terrible, that such as have been wicked men had rather be hanged than abide it. As Achitophel, that traitor to David, like an ambitious wretch, thought to have come to higher promotion, and therefore conspired with Absolon against his master David: he, when he saw his counsel took no place, goes and hangs himself, in contemplation of this evil-favoured face of death. Judas also, when he came with bushments to take his master Christ, in beholding this horrible face hanged himself. Yea, the elect people of God, the faithful, having the beholding of his face, (though God hath always preserved them, such a good God he is to them that believe in him, that 'he will not suffer them to be tempted above that that they have been able to bear,') yet for all that, there is nothing that they complain more sore than of this horror of death. Go to Job, what saith he? *Pereat dies in quo natus sum, suspendium elegit anima mea*; 'Wo worth the day that I was born in, my soul would be hanged': saying in his pangs almost he wist not what. This was when with the eye of his conscience and the inward man he beheld the horror of death and hell: not for any bodily pain he suffered; for when he had boils, blotches, blains, and scabs, he suffered them patiently: he could say then, *Si bona suscepi de manu Domini*, &c., 'If we have received good things of God, why should we not suffer likewise evil?' It was not for any such thing that he was so vexed: but the sight of this face of death and hell was offered to him so lively, that he would have been out of this world. It was this evil-favoured face of death that so troubled him. King David also said, in contemplation of this uglesome face, *Laboravi in gemitu meo*, 'I have been sore vexed with sighing and mourning.' *Turbatus est a furore oculus meus*, 'Mine eye hath been greatly troubled in my rage.' A strange thing! When he had to fight with Goliath, that monstrous giant, who was able to have eaten him, he could abide him, and was nothing afraid. And now what a work! What exclamations makes he at the sight of death! Jonas likewise was bold enough to bid the shipmen cast him into the sea, he had not seen that face and visage: but when he was in the whale's belly, and had there the beholding of it, what terror and distress abode he! Hezekiah, when he saw Sennacherib besieging his city on every side most violently, was nothing afraid of the great host and mighty army that was like to destroy him out of hand; yet he was afraid of death. When the prophet came unto him, and said, *Dispone domui tuæ, morte morieris et non vives*, 'Set thy house in order , for thou shalt surely die, and not live'; (2 Kings xx.), it struck him so to the heart that he fell a-weeping. O Lord, what an horror was this! There be some writers that say, that Peter, James, and John were in this feeling at the same time; and that Peter, when he said, *Exi a me, Domine, quia homo peccator sum*, 'Depart from me, O Lord, for I am a sinful man', did taste some part of it: he was so astonished, he wist not what to say. It was not long that they were in this anguish; some say longer, some shorter: but Christ was ready to comfort them, and said to Peter, *Ne timeas*, 'Be not afraid'. A friend of mine told me of a certain woman that was eighteen years together in it. I knew a man myself, Bilney, little Bilney, that blessed martyr of God, what time he had borne his fagot, and was come again to Cambridge, had such conflicts within himself, beholding the image of death, that his friends were afraid to let him be alone: they were fain to be with him day and night, and comforted him as they could, but no comforts would serve. As for the comfortable places of scripture, to bring them unto him it was as though a man would run him through the heart with a sword; yet afterward, for all this, he was revived, and took his death patiently, and died well against the tyrannical see of Rome. Wo will be to that bishop, that had the examination of him, if he repented not!

Here is a good lesson for you, my friends; if ever you come in danger, in durance, in prison for God's quarrel, and his sake, as he did for purgatory-matters, and put to bear a fagot for preaching the true word of God against pilgrimage, and such like matters, I will advise you first, and above all things, to abjure all your friends, all your friendships; leave not one unabjured. It is they that shall undo you, and not your enemies. It was his very friends that brought Bilney to it.

By this it may somewhat appear what our Saviour Christ suffered; he doth not dissemble it himself, when he saith, 'My soul is heavy to death': he was in so sore an agony, that there issued out of him, as I shall entreat anon, drops of blood. An ugsome thing surely, which this fact and deed sheweth us, what horrible pains he was in for our sakes! But you will say, 'How can this be? It were possible that I, and such other as be great sinners should suffer such affliction; the Son of God, what our Saviour Christ, [who] never sinned, how can this stand that he should be thus handled? He never deserved it.'

Marry, I will tell you how. We must consider our Saviour Christ two ways, one way in his manhood, another in his Godhead. Some places of scripture must be referred to his Deity, and some to his humanity. In his Godhead he suffered nothing; but now he made himself void of his Deity, as scripture saith, *Cum esset in forma Dei, exinanivit seipsum,* 'Whereas he was in the form of God, he emptied himself of it, he did hide it, and used himself as though he had not had it.' He would not help himself with his Godhead; 'he humbled himself with all obedience unto death, even to the death of the cross': this was in that he was man. He took upon him our sins: not the work of sin; I mean not so: not to do it, not to commit it; but to purge it, to cleanse it, to bear the stipend of it: and that way he was the great sinner of the world. He bare all the sin of the world on his back; he would become debtor for it.

Now to sustain and suffer the dolours of death is not to sin:

but he came into this world with his passion to purge our sins. Now this that he suffered in the garden is one of the bitterest pieces of all his passion: this fear of death was the bitterest pain that ever he abode, due to sin which he never did, but became debtor for us. All this he suffered for us; this he did to satisfy for our sins. It is much like as if I owed another man twenty thousand pounds, and should pay it out of hand, or else to the dungeon of Ludgate;[1] and when I am going to prison, one of my friends should come, and ask, 'Whither goeth this man?' and after he had heard the matter, should say, 'Let me answer for him, I will become surety for him: yea, I will pay all for him.' Such a part played our Saviour Christ with us. If he had not suffered this, I for my part should have suffered, according to the gravity and quantity of my sins, damnation. For the greater the sin is, the greater is the punishment in hell. He suffered for you and me, in such a degree as is due to all the sins of the whole world. It was as if you would imagine that one man had committed all the sins since Adam: you may be sure he should be punished with the same horror of death, in such a sort as all men in the world should have suffered. Feign and put case, our Saviour Christ had committed all the sins of the world; all that I for my part have done, all that you for your part have done, and that any man else hath done: if he had done all this himself, his agony that he suffered should have been no greater nor grievouser than it was. This that he suffered in the garden was a portion, I say, of his passion, and one of the bitterest parts of it. And this he suffered for our sins, and not for any sins that he had committed himself: for all we should have suffered, every man according to his own deserts. This he did of his goodness, partly to purge and cleanse our sins, partly because he would taste and feel our miseries, *quo possit succurrere nobis*, 'that he should the rather help and relieve us'; and partly he suffered to give us example to behave ourselves as he did. He did not suffer, to discharge us clean from death, to keep us clean from

1 Ludgate was the most western gate of the old city of London, to which was formerly attached a prison for all freemen of the city, imprisoned for debt.

it, not to taste of it. Nay, nay, you must not take it so. We shall
have the beholding of this ugsome face every one of us; we shall
feel it ourselves. Yet our Saviour Christ did suffer, to the intent
to signify to us that death is overcomeable. We shall indeed
overcome it, if we repent, and acknowledge that our Saviour
Jesu Christ pacified with his pangs and pains the wrath of the
Father; having a love to walk in the ways of God. If we believe
in Jesu Christ, we shall overcome death: I say it shall not prevail
against us. Wherefore, whensoever it chanceth thee, my friend,
to have the tasting of this death, that thou shalt be tempted with
this horror of death, what is to be done then? Whensover thou
feelest thy soul heavy to death, make haste and resort to this
garden; and with this faith thou shalt overcome this terror when
it cometh. Oh, it was a grievous thing that Christ suffered here!
O the greatness of this dolour that he suffered in the garden,
partly to make amends for our sins, and partly to deliver us
from death; not so that we should not die bodily, but that this
death should be a way to a better life, and to destroy and
overcome hell! Our Saviour Christ had a garden, but he had
little pleasure in it. You have many goodly gardens: I would
you would in the midst of them consider what agony our
Saviour Christ suffered in his garden. A goodly meditation to
have in your gardens! It shall occasion you to delight no farther
in vanities, but to remember what he suffered for you. It may
draw you from sin. It is a good monument, a good sign, a good
monition, to consider how he behaved himself in this garden.

Well; he saith to his disciples, 'Sit here and pray with me.' he
went a little way off, as it were a stone's cast from them, and
falleth to his prayer, and saith: *Pater, si possibile est, transeat a me
calix iste*; 'Father, if it be possible, away with this bitter cup, this
outrageous pain.' Yet after he corrects himself, and says,
Veruntamen non sicut ego volo, sed sicut tu vis; 'Not my will, but
thy will be done, O Father.' Here is a good meditation for
christian men at all times, and not only upon Good Friday. Let
Good Friday be every day to a christian man, to know to use his
passion to that end and purpose; not only to read the story, but
to take the fruit of it. Some men, if they had been in this agony,
would have run themselves through with their swords, as Saul

did: some would have hanged themselves, as Achitophel did. Let us not follow these men, they be no examples for us; but let us follow Christ, which in his agony resorted to his Father with his prayer. This must be our pattern to work by.

Here I might dilate the matter as touching praying to saints. Here we may learn not to pray to saints. Christ bids us, *Ora Patrem qui est in cœlis*, 'Pray to thy Father that is in heaven'; to the Creator, and not to any creature. And therefore away with these avowries: let God alone be our avowry.[1] What have we to do to run hither or thither, but only to the Father of heaven? I will not tarry to speak of this matter.

Our Saviour Christ set his disciples in an order, and commanded them to watch and pray, saying, *Vigilate et orate*; 'Watch and pray.' Whereto should they watch and pray? He saith by and by, *ne intretis in tentationem*, 'that ye enter not into temptation.' He bids them not pray that we be not tempted; for that is as much to say, as to pray that we should be out of this world. There is no man in this world without temptation. In the time of prosperity we are tempted to wantonness, pleasures, and all lightness; in time of adversity, to despair in God's goodness. Temptation never ceases. There is a difference between being tempted, and entering into temptation. He bids therefore not to pray that they be not tempted, but that they 'enter not into temptation.' To be tempted is no evil thing. For what is it? No more than when the flesh, the devil and the world, doth solicit and move us against God. To give place to these suggestions, and to yield ourselves, and suffer us to be overcome of them, this is to enter into temptation. Our Saviour Christ knew that they should be grievously tempted, and therefore he have them warning that they should not give place to temptation, nor despair at his death: and if they chanced to forsake him, or to run away, in case they tripped or swerved, yet to come again.

But our Saviour Christ did not only command his disciples to pray, but fell down upon his knees flat upon the ground, and prayed himself, saying, *Pater, si fieri potest, transeat a me calix iste*;

1 Protectors.

'Father, deliver me of this pang and pain that I am in, this outrageous pain.' This word, 'Father', came even from the bowels of his heart, when he made his moan; as who should say, 'Father, rid me; I am in such pain that I can be in no greater! Thou art my Father, I am thy Son. Can the Father forsake his son in such anguish? Thus he made his moan. 'Father, take away this horror of death from me; rid me of this pain; suffer me not to be taken when Judas comes; suffer me not to be hanged on the cross; suffer not my hands to be pierced with nails, nor my heart with the sharp spear.' A wonderful thing, that he should so oft tell his disciples of it before, and now, when he cometh to the point, to desire to be rid of it, as though he would have been disobedient to the will of his Father. Afore he said, he came to suffer; and now he says, away with this cup. Who would have thought that ever this gear should have come out of Christ's mouth? What a case is this! What should a man say? You must understand, that Christ took upon him our infirmities, of the which this was one, to be sorry at death. Among the stipends of sin, this was one, to tremble at the cross: this is a punishment for our sin.

It goeth otherways with us than with Christ: if we were in like case, and in like agony, almost we would curse God, or rather wish that there were no God. This that he said was not of that sort; it was referring the matter to the will of his Father. But we seek by all means, be it right, be it wrong, of our own nature to be rid out of pain: he desired it conditionally, as it might stand with his Father's will; adding a *veruntamen* to it. So his request was to shew the infirmity of man. Here is now an example what we shall do when we are in like case. He never deserved it, we have. He had a *veruntamen*, a notwithstanding: let us have so too. We must have a 'nevertheless, thy will be done, and not mine: give me grace to be content, to submit my will unto thine.' His fact teacheth us what to do. This is our surgery, our physic, when we be in agony: and reckon upon it, friends, we shall come to it; we shall feel it at one time or another.

What doth he now? What came to pass now, when he had heard no voice, his Father was dumb? He resorts to his friends, seeking some comfort at their hands. Seeing he had none at his

Father's hand, he cometh to his disciples, and finds them asleep. He spake unto Peter, and said, 'Ah Peter, art thou asleep?' Peter before had bragged stoutly, as though he would have killed, (God have mercy upon his soul!) and now, when he should have comforted Christ, he was asleep. Not once buff nor baff to him: not a word. He was fain to say to his disciples, *Vigilate et orate*, 'Watch and pray; the spirit is ready, but the flesh is weak': he had never a word of them again. They might at the least have said, 'O Sir, remember yourself; are you not Christ? Came not you into this world to redeem sin? Be of good cheer, be of good comfort: this sorrow will not help you; comfort yourself by your own preaching. You have said, *Oportet Filium hominis pati*, "It behoveth the Son of man to suffer." You have not deserved any thing, it is not your fault.' Indeed, if they had done this with him, they had played a friendly part with him; but they gave him not so much as one comfortable word. We run to our friends in our distresses and agonies, as though we had all our trust and confidence in them. He did not so; he resorted to them, but trusted not in them. We will run to our friends, and come no more to God; he returned again. What! Shall we not resort to our friends in time of need? And, trow ye, we shall not find them asleep? Yes, I warrant you: and when we need their help most, we shall not have it. But what shall we do, when we shall find lack in them? We will cry out upon them, upbraid them, chide, brawl, fume, chafe, and backbite them. But Christ did not so; he excused his friends, saying, *Vigilate et orate; spiritus quidem promptus est, caro autem infirma*: 'O!' quoth he, 'watch and pray: I see well the spirit is ready, but the flesh is weak.' What meaneth this? Surely it is a comfortable place. For as long as we live in this world, when we be at the best, we have no more but *promptitudinem spiritus cum infirmitate carnis*, the readiness of the spirit with the infirmity of the flesh. The very saints of God said, *Velle adest mihi*, 'My will is good, but I am not able to perform it.' I have been with some, and fain they would, fain they would: there was readiness of spirit, but it would not be; it grieved them that they could not take things as they should do. The flesh resisteth the work of the Holy Ghost in our hearts, and lets it, lets it. We have to pray ever to God. O prayer, prayer!

84

that it might be used in this realm, as it ought to be of all men, and specially of magistrates, of counsellors, of great rulers; to pray, to pray that it would please God to put godly policies in their hearts! Call for assistance.

I have heard say, when that good queen[1] that is gone had ordained in her house daily prayer both before noon, and after noon, the admiral gets him out of the way, like a mole digging in the earth. He shall be Lot's wife to me as long as I live. He was, I heard say, a covetous man, a covetous man indeed: I would there were no more in England! He was, I heard say, an ambitious man: I would there were no more in England! He was, I heard say, a seditious man, a contemner of common prayer: I would there were no more in England! Well: he is gone. I would he had left none behind him! Remember you, my lords, that you pray in your houses to the better mortification of your flesh: remember, God must be honoured. I will you to pray, that God will continue his Spirit in you. I do not put you in comfort, that if ye have once the Spirit, ye cannot lose it. There be new spirits start up now of late, that say after we have received the Spirit, we cannot sin.[2] I will make but one argument: St Paul had brought the Galatians to the profession of the faith, and left them in that state; they had received the Spirit once, but they sinned again, as he testified of them himself: he saith, *Currebatis bene*; ye were once in a right state: and again, *Recepistis Spiritum ex operibus legis an ex justitia fidei*? Once they had the Spirit by faith; but false prophets came, when he was gone from them, and they plucked them clean away from all that Paul had planted them in: and then said Paul unto them, *O stulti Galati, quis vos fascinavit*? 'O foolish Galatians, who hath bewitched you?' If this be true, we may lose the Spirit that we have once possessed. It is a fond thing: I will not tarry in it. But now to the passion again.

Christ had been with his Father, and felt no help: he had been with his friends, and had no comfort: he had prayed twice, and was not heard: what did he now? did he give prayer over? No,

1 Catherine Parr, who married the lord admiral Seymour.
2 The Familists, or followers of David George.

he goeth again to his Father, and saith the same again: 'Father, if it be possible, away with this cup.' Here is an example for us, although we be not heard at the first time, shall we give over our prayer? Nay, we must to it again. We must be instant in prayer. He prayed thrice, and was not heard; let us pray threescore times. Folks are very dull now-a-days in prayer, to come to sermons, to resort to common prayer. You house-keepers, and especially great men, give example of prayer in your houses.

Well; did his Father look upon him this second time? No, he went to his friends again, thinking to find some comfort there, but he finds them asleep again, more deep asleep than ever they were: their eyes were heavy with sleep; there was no comfort at all; they wist not what to say to him. A wonderful thing, how he was tost from post to pillar; one while to his Father, and was destitute at his hand; another while to his friends, and found no comfort at them: his Father gave him looking on, and suffered him to bite upon the bridle awhile. Almighty God beheld this battle, that he might enjoy the honour and glory; 'that in his name all knees should bow, *cœlestium, terrestrium et infernorum*, in heaven, earth, and hell. This, that the Father would not hear his own Son, was another punishment due to our sin. When we cry unto him, he will not hear us. The prophet Jeremy saith, *Clamabunt ad me et ego non exaudiam eos*; 'They shall cry unto me, and I will not hear them.' These be Jeremy's words: here he threateneth to punish sin with not hearing their prayers. The prophet saith, 'They have not had the fear of God before their eyes, nor have not regarded discipline and correction.' I never saw, surely, so little discipline as is now-a-days. Men will be masters; they will be masters and no disciples. Alas, where is this discipline now in England? The people regard no discipline; they be without all order. Where they should give place, they will not stir one inch: yea, where magistrates should determine matters, they will break into the place before they come, and at their coming not move a whit for them. Is this discipline? Is this good order? If a man say anything unto them, they regard it not. They that be called to answer, will not answer directly, but scoff the matter out. Men the more they know, the worse they be; it is truly said, *scientia inflat*, 'knowledge maketh us proud, and causeth us to forget all, and set away discipline.' Surely in popery they had a reverence; but now we have none at all. I never saw the like. This same lack of the fear of God and discipline in us was one of the causes that the Father would not hear his Son. This pain suffered our Saviour Christ for us, who never deserved it. O, what it was that he suffered in this garden, till Judas came! The dolours, the terrors, the sorrows that he suffered be unspeakable! He suffered partly to make amends for our sins, and partly to give us example, what we should do in like case. What comes of this gear in the end?

Well; now he prayeth again, he resorteth to his Father again. *Angore correptus prolixius orabat*: he was in sorer pains, in more anguish than ever he was; and therefore he prayeth longer, more ardently, more fervently, more vehemently, than ever he did before. O Lord, what a wonderful thing is this! This horror of death is worse than death itself, and is more ugsome. He prayeth now the third time. He did it so instantly, so fervently, that it brought out a bloody sweat, and in such plenty, that it dropped down even to the ground. There issued out of his precious body drops of blood. What a pain was he in, when these bloody drops fell so abundantly from him! Yet for all that, how unthankful do we shew ourselves toward him that died only for our sakes, and for the remedy of our sins! O what blasphemy do we commit day by day! what little regard have we to his blessed passion, thus to swear by God's blood, by Christ's passion! We have nothing in our pastime, but 'God's blood', 'God's wounds'. We continually blaspheme his passion, in hawking, in hunting, dicing, and carding. Who would think he should have such enemies among those that profess his name? What became of his blood that fell down, trow ye? Was the blood of Hales[1] of it? Wo worth it! What ado was there to bring this out of the king's head! This great abomination, of the blood of Hales, could not be taken a great while out of his mind.

You that be of the court, and especially ye sworn chaplains, beware of a lesson that a great man taught me at my first coming

1 A noted relic, kept in the abbey of Hales in Gloucestershire.

to the courts: he told me for good-will; he thought it well. He said to me, 'You must beware, howsoever ye do, that ye contrary not the king; let him have his sayings; follow him; go with him.' Marry, out upon this counsel! Shall I say as he says? Say your conscience, or else what a worm shall ye feel gnawing; what a remorse of conscience shall ye have, when ye remember how ye have slacked your duty! It is a good wise verse, *Gutta cavat lapidem non vi sed sæpe cadendo;* 'The drop of rain maketh a hole in the stone, not by violence, but by oft falling.' Likewise a prince must be turned; not violently, but he must be won by a little and a little. He must have his duty told him; but it must be done with humbleness, with request of pardon; or else it were a dangerous thing. Unpreaching prelates have been the cause, that the blood of Hales did so long blind the king. Wo worth that such an abominable thing should be in a christian realm! But thanks be to God, it was partly redressed in the king's days that dead is, and much more now. God grant good-will and power to go forward, if there be any such abomination behind, that it may be utterly rooted up!

O how happy are we, that it hath pleased Almighty God to vouchsafe that his Son should sweat blood for the redeeming of our sins! And, again, how unhappy are we, if we will not take it thankfully, that were redeemed so painfully! Alas, what hard hearts have we! Our Saviour Christ never sinned, and yet sweat the blood for our sins. We will not once water our eyes with a few tears. What an horrible thing is sin; that no other thing would remedy and pay the ransom for it, but only the blood of our Saviour Christ! There was nothing to pacify the Father's wrath against man, but such an agony as he suffered. All the passion of all the martyrs that ever were, all the sacrifices of patriarchs that ever were, all the good works that ever were done, were not able to remedy our sin, to make satisfaction for our sins, nor anything besides, but this extreme passion and blood-shedding of our most merciful Saviour Christ.

But to draw toward an end. What became of this three-fold prayer? At the length, it pleased God to hear his Son's prayer; and sent him an angel to corroborate, to strengthen, to comfort him. Christ needed no angel's help, if he had listed to ease himself with his deity. He was the Son of God: what then? Forsomuch as he was man, he received comfort at the angel's hand; as it accords to our infirmity. His obedience, his continuance, and suffering, so pleased the Father of heaven, that for his Son's sake, be he never so great a sinner, leaving his sin, and repenting for the same, he will owe him such favour as though he had never committed any sin. The Father of heaven will not suffer him to be tempted with this great horror of death and hell to the uttermost, and above that he is able to bear. Look for it, my friends, by him and through him, we shall be able to overcome it. Let us do as our Saviour Christ did, and we shall have help from above, we shall have angels' help: if we trust in him, heaven and earth shall give up, rather than we shall lack help. He saith he is *Adjutor in necessitatibus*, 'an helper in time of need.'

When the angel had comforted him, and when this horror of death was gone, he was so strong, that he offered himself to Judas; and said, 'I am he.' To make an end: I pray you take pains: it is a day of penance, as we use to say, give me leave to make you weary this day. The Jews had him to Caiaphas and Annas, and there they whipped him, and beat him: they set a crown of sharp thorns upon his head, and nailed him to a tree: yet all this was not so bitter, as this horror of death, and this agony that he suffered in the garden, in such a degree as is due to all the sins of the world, and not to one man's sins. Well; this passion is our remedy; it is the satisfaction of our sins.

His soul descended to hell for a time. Here is much ado! These new upstarting spirits say, 'Christ never descended into hell, neither body nor soul.' In scorn they will ask, 'Was he there? What did he there?' What if we cannot tell what he did there? The creed goeth no further, but saith, he descended thither. What is that to us, if we cannot tell, seeing we were taught no further? Paul was taken up into the third heaven; ask likewise what he saw when he was carried thither? You shall not find in scripture, what he saw or what he did there: shall we not, therefore, believe that he was there? These arrogant spirits, spirits of vain-glory, because they know not by any express scripture the order of his doings in hell, they will not believe that ever he descended into hell. Indeed this article hath not so full scripture, so many places and testimonies of scriptures, as others have; yet it hath enough: it hath two or three texts; and if it had but one, one text of scripture is of as good and lawful authority as a thousand, and of as certain truth. It is not to be weighed by the multitude of texts. I believe as certainly and verily that this realm of England hath as good authority to hear God's word, as any nation in all the world: it may be gathered by two texts: one of them is this; *Ite in universum mundum, et prædicate evangelium omni creatureæ*, 'Go into the whole world, and preach the gospel to all creatures.' Again, *Deus vult omnes homines salvos fieri*, 'God will have all men to be saved.' He excepts not the Englishmen here, nor yet expressly nameth them; and yet I am as sure that this realm of England, by this gathering, is allowed to hear God's word, as though Christ had said a thousand times, 'Go preach to Englishmen: I will that Englishmen be saved.' Because this article of his descending into hell cannot be gathered so directly, so necessarily, so formally, they utterly deny it.

This article hath scriptures two or three; enough for quiet minds: as for curious brains, nothing can content them. This the devil's stirring up of such spirits of sedition is an evident argument that the light is come forth; for his word is abroad when the devil rusheth, when he roareth, when he stirreth up such busy spirits to slander it. My intent is not to entreat of this matter at this time. I trust the people will not be carried away with these new arrogant spirits. I doubt not, but good preachers will labour against them.

But now I will say a word, and herein I protest first of all, not arrogantly to determine and define it: I will contend with no man for it; I will not have it to be prejudice to any body, but I offer it unto you to consider and weigh it. There be some great clerks[1] that take my part, and I perceive not what evil can come of it, in saying, that our Saviour Christ did not only in soul

1 The opinion here mentioned was maintained by Cardinal Nicholas de Cusa and other Romanists; and also by some of the continental reformers.

descend into hell, but also that he suffered in hell such pains as the damned spirits did suffer there. Surely, I believe verily, for my part, that he suffered the pains of hell proportionately, as it corresponds and answers to the whole sin of the world. He would not suffer only bodily in the garden and upon the cross, but also in his soul when it was from the body; which was a pain due for our sin. Some write so, and I can believe it, that he suffered in the very place, and I cannot tell what it is, call it what ye will, even in the scalding-house, in the ugsomeness of the place, in the presence of the place, such pain as our capacity cannot attain unto: it is somewhat declared unto us, when we utter it by these effects, 'by fire, by gnashing of teeth, by the worm that gnaweth on the conscience.' Whatsoever the pain is, it is a great pain that he suffered for us.

I see no inconvenience to say, that Christ suffered in soul in hell. I singularly commend the exceeding great charity of Christ, that for our sakes would suffer in hell in his soul. It sets out the unspeakable hatred that God hath to sin. I perceive not that it doth derogate any thing from the dignity of Christ's death; as in the garden, when he suffered, it derogates nothing from that he suffered on the cross. Scripture speaketh on this fashion: *Qui credit in me habet vitam œternam;* 'He that believeth in me, hath life everlasting.' Here he sets forth faith as the cause of our justification; in other places, as high commendation is given to works: and yet, are the works any derogation from that dignity of faith? No. And again, Scripture saith, *Traditus est propter peccata nostra, et exsuscitatus propter justificationem,* &c. It attributeth here our justification to his resurrection; and doth this derogate any thing from his death? Not a whit. It is whole Christ. What with his nativity; what with his circumcision; what with his incarnation and the whole process of his life; with his preaching; what with his ascending, descending; what with his death; it is all Christ that worketh our salvation. He sitteth on the right hand of the Father, and all for us. All this is the work of our salvation. I would be as loth to derogate any thing from Christ's death, as the best of you all. How inestimably are we bound to him! What thanks ought we to give him for it! We must have this continually in remembrance: *Propter te morti tradimur tota die,* 'For there we are in dying continually.' The life of a christian man is nothing but a readiness to die, and a remembrance of death.

If this that I have spoken of Christ's suffering in the garden, and in hell, derogate any thing from Christ's death and passion, away with it; believe me not in this. If it do not, it commends and sets forth very well unto us the perfection of the satisfaction that Christ made for us, and the work of redemption, not only before witness in this world, but in hell, in that ugsome place; where whether he suffered or wrestled with the spirits, or comforted Abraham, Isaac, and Jacob, I will not desire to know. If ye like not that which I have spoken of his suffering, let it go, I will not strive in it: I will be prejudice to no body, weigh it as ye list. I do but offer it to you to consider. It is like, his soul did somewhat the three days that his body lay in the grave. To say, he suffered in hell for us, derogates nothing from his death: for all things that Christ did before his suffering on the cross, and after, do work our salvation, If he had not been incarnate, he had not died: he was beneficial to us with all things he did. Christian people should have his suffering for them in remembrance. Let your gardens monish you, your pleasant gardens, what Christ suffered for you in the garden, and what commodity you have by his suffering. It is his will ye should so do; he would be had in remembrance. Mix your pleasures with the remembrance of his bitter passion. The whole passion is satisfaction for our sins; and not the bare death, considering it so nakedly by itself. The manner of speaking of scripture is to be considered. It attributeth our salvation now to one thing, now to another that Christ did; where indeed it pertained to all. Our Saviour Christ hath left behind him a remembrance of his passion, the blessed communion, the celebration of the Lord's Supper: alack! it hath been long abused, as the sacrifices were before in the old law. The patriarchs used sacrifice in the faith of the Seed of the woman, which should break the serpent's head. The patriarchs sacrificed on hope, and afterward the work was esteemed. There come other after, and they consider not the faith of Abraham and the patriarchs, but do their sacrifice according to their own imagination: even so came it to pass with our blessed communion. In the primitive church, in places when their friends were dead, they used to come together to the holy communion.[1] What! to remedy them that were dead? No, no, a straw; it was instituted for no such purpose. But then they would call to remembrance God's goodness, and his passion that he suffered for us, wherein they comforted much their faith.

Others came afterward, and set up all these kinds of massing, all these kinds of iniquity. What an abomination is it, the foulest that ever was, to attribute to man's work our salvation! God be thanked that we have this blessed communion set forth so now, that we may comfort, increase, and fortify our faith at that blessed celebration! If he be guilty of the body of Christ, that takes it unworthily; he fetcheth great comfort at it, that eats it worthily. He doth eat it worthily, that doth eat it in faith. In faith? in what faith? Not long ago a great man said in an audience, 'They babble much of faith; I will go lie with my whore all night, and have as good a faith as the best of them all.' I think he never knew other but the whoremonger's faith. It is no such faith that will serve. It is no bribing judge's or justice's faith; no rent-raiser's faith; no whoremonger's faith; no lease-monger's faith; nor no seller of benefices' faith; but the faith in the passion of our Saviour Christ. We must believe that our Saviour Christ hath taken us again to his favour, that he hath delivered us his own body and blood, to plead with the devil, and by merit of his own passion, of his own mere liberality. This is the faith, I tell you, that we must come to the communion with, and not the whoremonger's faith. Look where remission of sin is, there is acknowledging of sin also. Faith is a noble duchess, she hath ever her gentleman-usher going before her, – the confessing of sins: she hath a train after her, – the fruits of good works, the walking in the commandments of God. He that

1 In the first Prayer Book of Edward VI, the third part of the Burial Service consisted of 'The celebration of the Holy Communion when there is a burial of the dead.' This, though omitted at the revision of the Prayer Book in 1552, was yet incorporated into the Latin Prayer published, chiefly for the use of the universities and public schools, in the second year of the reign of Queen Elizabeth.

believeth will not be idle, he will walk; he will do his business. Have ever the gentleman-usher with you. So if ye will try faith, remember this rule, – consider whether the train be waiting upon her. If you have another faith than this, a whoremonger's faith, you are like to go to the scalding-house, and there you will have two dishes, weeping and gnashing of teeth. Much good it do you! you see your fare. If ye will believe and acknowledge your sins, you shall come to the blessed communion of the bitter passion of Christ worthily, and so attain to everlasting life: to the which the Father of heaven bring you and me! *Amen.*

The Last Sermon Preached Before Edward VI
(Lent 1550)

[...] I have now preached three Lents. The first time I preached restitution. 'Restitution,' quoth some, 'what should he preach of restitution? Let him preach of contrition,' quoth they, 'and let restitution alone; we can never make restitution.' Then, say I, if thou wilt not make restitution, thou shalt go to the devil for it. Now choose thee either restitution, or else endless damnation. But now there be two manner of restitutions; secret restitution, and open restitution: whether of both it be, so that restitution be made, it is all good enough. At my first preaching of restitution, one good man took remorse of conscience, and acknowledged himself to me, that he had deceived the king; and willing he was to make restitution: and so the first Lent came to my hands twenty pounds to be restored to the king's use. I was promised twenty pound more the same Lent, but it could not be made, so that it came not. Well, the next Lent came three hundred and twenty pounds more. I received it myself, and paid it to the king's council. So I was asked, what he was that made this restitution? But should I have named him? Nay, they should as soon have this wesant[1] of mine. Well, now this Lent came one hundred and fourscore pounds ten shillings, which I have paid and delivered this present day to the king's council: and so this man hath made a godly restitution. 'And so,' quoth I to a certain nobleman that is one of the king's council, 'if every man that hath beguiled the king should make restitution after this sort, it would cough the king twenty thousand pounds, I think,' quoth I. 'Yea, that it would,' quoth the other, 'a whole hundred thousand pounds.' Alack, alack; make restitution; for God's sake make restitution: ye will cough

1 Wind-pipe.

in hell else, that all the devils there will laugh at your coughing. There is no remedy, but restitution open or secret; or else hell.

This that I have now told you of was a secret restitution. Some examples that been of open restitution, and glad may he be that God was so friendly unto him, to bring him unto it in this world. I am not afraid to name him; it was Master Sherington,[1] an honest gentleman, and one that God loveth. He openly confessed that he had deceived the king, and he made open restitution. Oh, what an argument may he have against the devil, when he shall move him to desperation! God brought this out to his amendment. It is a token that he is a chosen man of God, and one of his elected. If he be of God, he shall be brought to it: therefore for God's sake make restitution, or else remember God's proverb; 'There is nothing so secret,' &c. If you do either of these two in this world, then are ye of God; if not, then for lack of restitution, ye shall have eternal damnation. Ye may do it by means, if you dare not do it yourselves; bring it to another, and so make restitution. If ye be not of God's flock, it shall be brought out to your shame and damnation at the last day; when all evil men's sins shall be laid open before us. Yet there is one way, how all our sins may be hidden, which is, repent and amend. *Recipiscentia, recipiscentia*, repenting and amending is a sure remedy, and a sure way to hide all, that it shall not come out to our shame and confusion.

Yet there was another seed that Christ was sowing in that sermon of his; and this was the seed: 'I say to you, my friends, fear not him that killeth the body, but fear him that after he hath killed, hath power also to cast into hell-fire,' &c. And there, to put his disciples in comfort and sure hope of his help, and out of all doubt and mistrust of his assistance, he bringeth in unto them the example of the sparrows, how they are fed by God's mere providence and goodness; and also of the hairs of our heads, how that not so much as one hair falleth from our heads

---

1 Sir William Sherington, Vice-Treasurer of the Mint at Bristol, had, while in office, coined a large quantity of testers of base alloy and under standard value, by which he enriched himself, but defrauded the government and country.

without him. 'Fear him,' saith he, 'that when he hath killed the body, may also cast into hell-fire.' Matter for all kinds of people here, but specially for kings. And, therefore, here is another suit to your Highness. 'Fear not him that killeth the body.' Fear not these foreign princes and foreign powers. God shall make you strong enough. Stick to God: fear God, fear not them. God hath sent you many storms in your youth; but forsake not God, and he will not forsake you. Peradventure ye shall have that shall move you, and say unto you, 'Oh, Sir! Oh, such a one is a great man, he is a mighty prince, a king of great power, ye cannot be without his friendship, agree with him in religion, or else ye shall have him your enemy,' &c. Well, fear them not, but cleave to God, and he shall defend you. Do not as king Ahaz did, that was afraid of the Assyrian king, and for fear lest he should have him to his enemy, was content to forsake God, and to agree with him in religion and worshipping of God: and anon went to Urias the high priest, who was ready at once to set up the idolatry of the Assyrian king. Do not your Highness so: fear not the best of them all; but fear God. The same Urias was *capellanus ad manum*, 'a chaplain at hand', an elbow chaplain. If ye will turn, ye shall have that will turn with you; yea, even in their white rochets. But follow not Ahaz. Remember the hair, how it falleth not without God's providence. Remember the sparrows, how they build in every house, and God provideth for them. 'And ye are much more precious to me,' saith Christ, 'than sparrows or other birds.' God will defend you; that before your time cometh, ye shall not die nor miscarry.

On a time when Christ was going to Jerusalem, his disciples said unto him, 'They there would have stoned thee, and wilt thou now go thither again?' What saith he again to them? *Nonne duodecim sunt horæ die*, &c., 'Be there not twelve hours in the day?' saith he: God hath appointed his times, as pleaseth him; and before the time cometh that God hath appointed, they shall have no power against you. Therefore stick to God and forsake him not; but fear him, and fear not men. And beware chiefly of two affections, fear and love: fear, as Ahaz, of whom I have told you, that for fear of the Assyrian king he changed his religion, and thereby purchased God's high indignation to him and to his realm; and love, as Dina, Jacob's daughter, who caused a change of religion by Sichem and Hemor, who were contented for lust of a wife to the destruction and spoiling of all the whole city. Read the chronicles of England and France, and ye shall see what changes of religion hath come by marriages, and for marriages. 'Marry my daughter, and be baptized, and so forth, or else.' Fear them not. Remember the sparrows. And this rule should all estates and degrees of men follow; whereas now they fear men and not God. If there be a judgment between a great man and a poor man, then must there be a corruption of justice for fear. 'Oh, he is a great man, I dare not displease him.' Fie upon thee! art thou a judge, and wilt be afraid to give right judgment? Fear him not, be he never so great a man; but uprightly do true justice. Likewise some pastors go from their cure; they are afraid of the plague, they dare not come nigh any sick body, but hire others; and they go away themselves. Out upon thee! The wolf cometh upon thy flock to devour them, and when they have most need of thee, thou runnest away from them! The soldier also, that should go on warfare, he will draw back as much as he can. 'Oh I shall be slain! Oh, such and such went, and never came home again. Such men went the last year into Norfolk, and were slain there.' Thus they are afraid to go: they will labour to tarry at home. If the king command thee to go, thou art bound to go; and serving the king thou servest God. If thou serve God, he will not shorten thy days to thine hurt. 'Well,' saith some, 'if they had not gone, they had lived unto this day.' How knowest thou that? Who made thee so privy of God's counsel? Follow thou thy vocation, and serve the king when he calleth thee. In serving him thou shalt serve God; and till thy time come, thou shalt not die. It was marvel that Jonas escaped in such a city: what then? Yet God preserved him, so that he could not perish. Take therefore an example of Jonas, and every man follow his vocation, not fearing men, but fearing God.

Another seed that Christ was sowing in the sermon was this: *Qui confessus me fuerit hominibus, confiteboret ego illum coram Patre meo*; 'He that confesseth me before men, I shall also confess him before my Father.' We must confess him with mouth. It was of a bishop not long ago asked as touching this: 'laws,' saith he, 'must be obeyed, and civil ordinance I will follow outwardly; but my heart in religion is free to think as I will.' So said Friar Forest,[1] half a papist, yea, worse than a whole papist.

Well, another seed was, 'He that sinneth against the Holy Ghost, it shall not be forgiven him, neither in this world nor in the world to come.' What is this same sin against the Holy Ghost, an horrible sin that never shall be forgiven, neither in this world nor in the world to come? What is this sin? Final impenitency: and some say, impugning of the truth. One came to me once, that despaired because of sin against the Holy Ghost. He was sore troubled in his conscience, that he should be damned; and that it was not possible for him to be saved, because he had sinned against the Holy Ghost. I said to him, 'What, man,' quoth I, 'comfort yourself in these words of the apostle, *Christus est propitiatio pro peccatis nostris*:[2] and again; *Ideo me misit Pater in mundum, ut qui credit in me non pereat, sed habeat vitam æternam*; "My Father hath for this purpose sent me into the world, that he which believeth in me may not perish, but may have the life everlasting." Also, *Quacunque hora ingemuerit peccator salvus erit*; "In what hour soever the sinner shall mourn for his sin, he shall be saved."' I had scriptures enough for me, as methought; but say what I could say, he could say more against himself, than I could say at that time to do him good withal. Where some say that the sin against the Holy Ghost is original sin; I alleged against that the saying of St Paul, *Sicut per unius delictum*, &c., and *si quis egerit pœnitentiam*; 'If a man had done all the sins in the world, and have true repentance, with faith and hope in God's mercy, he shall be forgiven.' But whatsoever I said, he could still object against me, and avoid my reasons. I was fain to take another day, and did so. 'Let me go to my book,' quoth I, 'and go you to your prayers, for ye are not altogether without faith.' I got me to my study; I read many

---

1 John Forest, a Friar Observant and confessor to Queen Katharine, the first wife of Henry VIII. He was executed in 1538 for writing against the supremacy of the crown.
2 Christ is the propitiation for our sins.

doctors, but none could content me; no expositor could please me, nor satisfy my mind in the matter. And it is with me as it was with a scholar of Cambridge, who being demanded of his tutor how he understood his lesson, and what it meant, 'I know,' quoth he, 'what it meaneth, but I cannot tell it; I cannot express it.' So I understand it well enough, but I cannot well declare it. Nevertheless I will bungle at it as well as I can.

Now to tell you, by the way, what sin it was that he had committed: he had fallen from the truth known, and afterward fell to mocking and scorning of it; and this sin it was that he thought to be unforgiveable. I said unto him, that it was a vehement manner of speaking in scripture; 'Yet,' quoth I, 'this is not spoken universally; nor it is not meant that God doth never forgive it; but it is commonly called irremissible, unforgiveable, because that God doth seldom forgive it. But yet there is not sin so great but God may forgive it, and doth forgive it to the repentant heart, though in words it sound that it shall never be forgiven: as, *privilegium paucorum non destruit regulam universalem*, The privilege of a few persons doth not destroy an universal rule or saying of scripture. For the scripture saith, *Omnes moriemur*, 'We shall die every one of us': yet some shall be rapt and taken alive, as St Paul saith; for this privilege of a few doth not hurt a generality. An irremissible sin, an unexcusable sin; yet to him that will truly repent, it is forgiveable; in Christ it may be remitted. If there be no more but one man forgiven, ye may be that same one man that shall be forgiven: *Ubi abundavit delictum, ibi abundavit et gratia*; 'Where iniquity hath abounded, there shall grace abound.' Thus by little and little this man came to a settled conscience again, and took comfort in Christ's mercy. Therefore despair not, though it be said it shall never be forgiven. Where Cain said, 'My wickedness is so great that God cannot forgive it'; Nay, thou liest, saith Austin to Cain, *Major est Dei misericordia, quam iniquitas tua*; 'The mercy of God is greater than thine iniquity.' Therefore despair not; but this one thing I say: beware of this sin that ye fall not into it; for I have known no more but this one man, that hath fallen from the truth, and hath afterward repented and come to grace again. I have known many since

God hath opened my eyes to see a little; I have known many, I say, that knew more than I, and some whom I have honoured, that have afterwards fallen from the truth; but never one of them, this man except, that have returned to grace and to the truth again. But yet, though God doth very seldom forgive this sin, and although it be one of the sins that God doth hate most of all others, and such as is almost never forgiven, yet it is forgiveable in the blood of Christ, if one truly repent; and lo! it is universal. As there is also another scripture, *Væ terræ cujus rex puer est*, 'Wo be to the land, to the realm whose king is a child'; which some interpret and refer to childish conditions: but it is commonly true the other way too, when it is referred to the age and years of childhood. For where the king is within age, they that have governance about the king have much liberty to live voluptuously and licentiously; and not to be in fear how they govern, as they would be if the king were of full age; and then commonly they govern not well. But yet Josias and one or two more, though they were children, yet had their realms well governed, and reigned prosperously; and yet the saying, *Væ terræ cujus rex puer est*, is nevertheless true for all that. And this I gather of this irremissible sin against the Holy Ghost, that the scripture saith it is never forgiven, because it is seldom forgiven. For indeed I think that there is no sin, which God doth so seldom nor so hardly forgive, as this sin of falling away from the truth, after that a man once knoweth it. And indeed this took best place with the man that I have told you of, and best quieted his conscience.

Another seed was this: 'Be not careful,' saith Christ, 'what ye shall say before judge and magistrates, when ye are brought afore them for my name's sake; for the Holy Ghost shall put in your minds, even at that present hour, what ye shall speak.' A comfortable saying, and a goodly promise of the Holy Ghost, that 'the adversaries of the truth,' saith he, 'shall not be able to resist us.' What? shall the adversaries of the truth be dumb? Nay; there be no greater talkers, nor boasters, and facers[1] than they be. But they shall not be able to resist the truth to destroy it.

1 Putters-on of a bold appearance.

Here some will say, 'What needeth universities then, and the preservation of schools? The Holy Ghost will give always what to say.' Yea, but for all that we may not tempt God; we must trust in the Holy Ghost, but we must not presume on the Holy Ghost. Here now should I speak of universities, and for preferring of schools: but he that preached the last Sunday spake very well in it, and substantially, and like one that knew the state and condition of the universities and schools very well. But thus much I say unto you, magistrates: if ye will not maintain schools and universities, ye shall have a brutality. Therefore now a suit again to your Highness. So order the matter, that preaching may not decay: for surely, if preaching decay, ignorance and brutishness will enter again. Nor give the preachers' livings to secular men. What should the secular men do with the livings of preachers? I think there be at this day ten thousand students less than were within these twenty years, and fewer preachers; and that is the cause of rebellion. If there were good bishops, there should be no rebellion.

I am now almost come to my matter, saving one saying of Christ which was another seed: *Date, et dabitur vobis*; 'Give, and it shall be given unto you', &c. But who believeth this? If men believed this promise, they would give more than they do; and at leastwise they would not stick to give a little: but now-a-days men's study is set rather to take gifts, and to get of other men's goods, than to give any of their own. So all other the promises are mistrusted and unbelieved. For if the rich men did believe this promise of God, they would willingly and readily give a little to have the overplus. So where Christ saith of injuries, or offences and trespasses, *Mihi vindicta, et ego retribuam*, &c., 'Leave the avenging of wrongs alone unto me, and I shall pay them home', &c.: if the rebels had believed this promise, they would not have done as they did. So all the promises of God are mistrusted. Noah also after the flood feared at every rain lest the world should be drowned and destroyed again; till God gave the rainbow. And what exercise shall we have by the rainbow? We may learn by the rainbow, that God will be true of his promises, and will fulfil his promises. For God sent the rainbow; and four thousand years it is, and more, since this promise was made, and yet God hath been true of his promise unto this day: so that now when we see the rainbow, we may learn that God is true of his promise. And as God was true in this promise, so is he and will be in all the rest. But the covetous man doth not believe that God is true of his promise; for if he did, he would not stick to give of his goods to the poor. But as touching that I spake afore, when we see the rainbow, and see in the rainbow that that is like water, and of a watery colour, and as we may and ought not only to take thereof hold and comfort of God's promise, that he will no more destroy the world with water for sin; but also we may take an example to fear God, who in such wise hateth sin: likewise when in the rainbow we see that it is of a fiery colour, and like unto fire, we may gather an example of the end of the world, that except we amend, the world shall at last be consumed with fire for sin; and to fear the judgment of God, after which they that are damned shall be burned in hell-fire. These were the seeds that Christ was sowing, when this covetous man came unto him.

And now I am come to my matter. While Christ was thus preaching, this covetous fellow would not tarry till all the sermon was done, but interrupted the sermon; even suddenly chopping in, 'Master,' quoth he, 'speak to my brother, that he may divide the inheritance with me.' He would not abide till the end of the sermon; but his mind was on his halfpenny; and he would needs have his matter despatched out of hand. 'Master,' quoth he, 'let my brother divide with me.' Yet this was a good fellow: he could be contented with part, he desired not to have all together alone to himself, but could be content with a division, and to have his part of the inheritance. And what was the inheritance? *Ager*; a field: so that it was but one piece of ground, or one farm. This covetous man could be content with the half of one farm, where our men now-a-days cannot be satisfied with many farms at once. One man must now have as many farms as will serve many men, or else he will not be contented nor satisfied. They will jar now-a-days one with another, except they have all. 'Oh,' saith the wise man, 'there be three things wherein my soul delighteth: *Concordia fratrum, amor proximorum, et vir ac mulier bene sibi consentientes*; the unity

103

of brethren, the love of neighbours, and a man and wife agreeing well together.' So that the concord of brethren, and agreeing of brethren, is a gay thing. What saith Salomon of his matter? *Frater qui adjuvatur a fratre quasi civitas firma et turris fortis*; 'The brother that is holpen of his brother, is a sure and well-fenced city, and a strong tower,' he is so strong. Oh, it is a great matter, when brethren love and hold well together! But if the one go about to pull down the other, then are they weak both of them; and when one pulleth down his fellow, they must needs down both of them; there is no stay to hold them up.

Mark in the chronicles of England. Two brethren have reigned jointly together, the one on this side Humber, and the other beyond Humber, in Scotland, and all that way. And what hath come of it? So long as they have agreed well together, so long they have prospered; and when they have jarred, they have both gone to wrack.[1] Brethren that have so reigned here in England, have quarrelled one with another; and the younger hath not been contented with his portion,[2] (as indeed the younger brother commonly jarreth first) but by the contention both have fared the worse. So when there is any contention between brother and brother for land, commonly they are both undone by it. And that crafty merchant, whatever he be, that will set brother against brother, meaneth to destroy them both. But of these two brethren, whether this man here were the elder or the younger; for once it was a plain law, that *primogenitus*, that is to say, the elder brother, had *duplicia*;[3] and therefore of likelihood it should be the youngest brother that found himself aggrieved, and was not content. But Christ said unto him, 'Thou man, who hath made me a judge or a divider between you?' Christ answered him by a question; and mark this question of Christ, 'Thou man,' *Quis me constituit judicem aut divisorem super vos*; 'Who made me a judge', &c. It is no small matter, saith

1 The allusion seems to be to the dissensions between the kingdoms of Northumbria and Deira.
2 The Wars of the Roses, and the usurpation of Richard III, were the result of the younger not being 'contented with his portion', as was, also, the execution of the lord admiral Seymour.
3 Double claim.

104

Augustine,[1] of what intention one asketh a question; as Christ in another place of the gospel asketh who was neighbour to the pilgrim that was wounded. 'There was,' saith Christ, 'a man that went from Jerusalem to Jericho, and fell among thieves, and they wounded him, and left him for dead. And a priest came by, that was his own countryman, and let him lie; a Levite came by, and would shew no compassion upon him: at last a Samaritan came by, and set him on his horse, and conveyed him to the city, and provided surgery for him, &c. Now who was neighbour to this wounded man?' saith Christ. *Qui fecit illi misericordiam*, quoth the lawyer; 'He that shewed mercy unto him.' He that did the office of a neighbour, he was a neighbour. As ye may perceive by a more familiar example of the bishop of Exeter[2] at Sutton in Staffordshire. Who is bishop of Exeter? Forsooth, Master Coverdale. What, do not all men know who is bishop of Exeter? What? He hath been bishop many years. Well, say I, Master Coverdale is bishop of Exeter: Master Coverdale putteth in execution the bishop's office, and he that doth the office of the bishop, he is the bishop indeed: therefore say I, Master Coverdale is bishop of Exeter. Alack! there is a thing that maketh my heart sorry. I hear that Master Coverdale is poisoned. Alack! a good man, a godly preacher, an honest fatherly man; and, if it be true, it is a great pity and a lamentable case, that he feeding them with God's word, they should feed him again with poison.

But to the purpose of Christ's question, 'Who made me a judge between you?' Here an Anabaptist will say, 'Ah! Christ refused the office of a judge; *ergo* there ought to be no judges nor magistrates among christian men. If it had been a thing lawful, Christ would not have refused to do the office of a judge, and to have determined the variance between these two

1 On the Gospel of John, c. 5, Tract xix.
2 John Voysey or Harman, who lived chiefly at Sutton Coldfield in Warwickshire, leaving the episcopal duties of the diocese of Exeter to be discharged by the well-known Miles Coverdale, then bishop Voysey's coadjutor, and afterwards his successor in the see of Exeter.

brethren.' But Christ did thereby signify that he was not sent for that office; but if thou will have a trial and a sentence of that matter according to the laws, thou must go to the temporal judge that is deputed therefor. But Christ's meaning was, that he was come for another purpose; he had another office deputed unto him than to be a judge in temporal matters. *Ego veni vocare peccatores ad pœnitentiam*; 'I am come,' saith he, 'to call sinners to repentance': he was come to preach the gospel, the remission of sin, and the kingdom of God; and meant not thereby to disallow the office of temporal magistrates. Nay, if Christ had meant that there should be no magistrates, he would have bid him take all: but Christ meant nothing so. But the matter is, that this covetous man, this brother, took his mark amiss; for he came to a wrong man to seek redress of his matter. For Christ did not forbid him to seek his remedy at the magistrate's hand; but Christ refused to take upon him the office that was not his calling. For Christ had another vocation than to be a judge between such as contended about matters of land. If our rebels had had this in their minds, they would not have been their own judges; but they would have sought the redress of their grief at the hands of the king, and his magistrates under him appointed. But no marvel of their blindness and ignorance; for the bishops are out of their dioceses that should teach them this gear. But this man perchance had heard, and did think that Christ was Messias, whose reign in words soundeth a corporal and a temporal reign; which should do justice and see a redress in all matters of worldly controversy: which is a necessary office in a christian realm, and must needs be put in execution for ministering of justice. And therefore I require you, as a suitor rather than a preacher, look to your office yourself, and lay not all on your officers' backs; receive the bills of supplication yourself: I do not see you do so now-a-days as ye were wont to do the last year. For God's sake look unto it, and see to the ministering of justice your own self, and let poor suitors have answer. There is a king in Christendom, and it is the king of Denmark,[1] that sitteth

1 Christian III, of whom it was said that 'he was equally the father of

openly in justice thrice in the week, and hath doors kept open for the nones.[1] I have heard it reported of one that hath been there, and seen the proof of it many a time and oft: and the last justice that ever he saw done there, was of a priest's cause that had had his glebe land taken from him, (and now here in England some go about to take away all;) but his priest had had his glebe land taken from him by a great man. Well; first went out letters for this man to appear at a day: process went out for him according to the order of the law, and charged him by virtue of those letters to appear afore the king at such a day. The day came: the king sat in his hall ready to minister justice. The priest was there present. The gentleman, this lord, this great man, was called, and commanded to make his appearance according to the writ that had been directed out for him. And the lord came, and was there; but he appeared not. 'No,' quoth the king, 'was he summoned as he should be? Had he any warning to be here?' It was answered, 'Yea; and that he knew well enough that that was his day; and also, that he had already been called; but he said, he would not come before the king at that time: alleging that he needed not as yet to make an answer, because he had had but one summoning.' 'No,' quoth the king, 'is he here present?' 'Yea, forsooth, sir,' said the priest. The king commanded him to be called, and to come before him: and the end was this, he made this lord, this great man, to restore unto the priest not only the glebe land which he had taken from the priest, but also the rent and profit thereof for so long time as he had withholden it from the priest; which was eight years or thereabout. Saith he, 'When you can shew better evidence than the priest hath done, why it ought to be your land, then he shall restore it to you again, and the profits thereof that he shall receive in the mean time: but till that day come, I charge ye that ye suffer him peaceably to enjoy that is his.'

This is a noble king; and this I tell for your example, that ye

all his subjects, and of his own family'. It was by this sovereign that the Reformation in Denmark was finally settled.

1 Purpose.

may do the like. Look upon the matter yourself. Poor men put up bills every day, and never the near. Confirm your kingdom in judgment; and begin doing of your own office yourself, even now while you are young, and sit once or twice in the week in council among your lords: it shall cause things to have good success, and that matters shall not be lingered forth from day to day. It is good for every man to do his own office, and to see that well executed and discharged.

Ozias king in Juda, he would needs do the office of the priest, and he would needs offer incense in the sanctuary; which to do was the priest's office. But he was suddenly stricken with the leprosy for his labour, and so continued a leper all the days of his life. St John's disciples would have had their master to take upon him that he was Christ. But what said John? *Nemo sibi assumit quicquam nisi datum fuerit ei desuper*; 'No man may take any thing upon himself, except it be given unto him from above.' If the Devonshire men had well considered this, they had not provoked the plagues that they have had light upon them. But unpreaching prelacy hath been the chiefest cause of all this hurly-burly and commotions. But if Christ may challenge any kind of men for taking his office upon them, he may say to the mass-mongers, 'Who gave you commission to offer up Christ? Who gave you authority to take mine office in hand?' For it is only Christ's office to do that. It is a greater matter to offer Christ. If Christ had offered his body at the last supper, then should we so do too. Who is worthy to offer up Christ? An abominable presumption! Paul saith, *Accepit panem; postquam gratias egisset, fregit, et dixit, Accipite, edite*; 'He took bread, and after that he had given thanks, he brake it, and said, Take ye, eat ye', &c.: and so said, *Hoc est corpus meum*, 'This is my body.' He gave thanks? Well then: in thanksgiving there is no oblation; and when he gave thanks, it was not his body.

When I was in examination,[1] I was asked many questions, and it was said to me, What Christ did, that should we do: a bishop gathered that upon these words, *Hoc facite in mei*

1 Latimer is probably referring to his examination before the Council, 14 May 1546.

recordationem, 'Do this in remembrance of me.' Then said he to me, 'How know ye that they ate it, before he said, *Hoc est corpus meum*, "This is my body"?' I answered again and said, 'How know ye that they did not it?' &c. So I brought unto him the place of Paul above said; and that in thanksgiving is none oblation; and when he gave thanks it was not his body, for he gave thanks in the beginning of supper, before they eat any manner of thing at all; as his accustomed manner was to do. I wonder therefore, that they will or dare by this text take upon them to offer Christ's body: they should rather say, *Quis me constituit oblatorem*, 'Who made me an offerer?' But when Christ said, *Quis me constituit judicem aut divisorem super vos*, 'Who hath made me a judge or a divider of lands among you?' Christ did refuse another man's office; an office that he was not of his Father deputed unto. Christ's kingdom was a spiritual kingdom, and his office was a spiritual office; and he was a spiritual judge. And therefore, when the woman taken in adultery was brought before him, he refused not to play the judge; but said, *Quis te accusat*, 'Who accuseth thee?' and she said again, *Nemo, Domine*: 'No man, Lord.' Then said he, *Nec ego te condemno*, 'Nor I condemn thee not.' *Vade et noli amplius peccare*, 'Go thy ways, and sin no more.' Here he took upon him his own office, and did his office; for his office was to preach, and bid sinners amend their evil living, and not to be a temporal judge in temporal causes. And here is another occasion of a suit to your highness, for the punishment of lechery; for lechery floweth in England like a flood.

But now to make an end in temporal causes. He said, *Quis me constituit judicem*, &c., 'Who made me a judge of temporal causes among you, and of worldly matters?' Thus came this fellow in here with interrupting of Christ's sermon, and received the answer which I have rehearsed. 'Thou man, thou fellow,' quoth he, 'who hath made me a judge among you?' And he said unto all the audience, *Videte et cavete ab avaritia*; 'See and beware of covetousness.' Why so? *Quia non in abundantia cujusquam vita ejus est ex his quæ possidet*; 'For no man's life standeth in the abundance of the things which he possesseth.' We may have things necessary, and we may have abundance of things; but the abundance doth not make us blessed. It is not good argument, *Quo plus quisque habet, tanto beatius vivit*; 'The more riches that a man hath, the more happily and the more blissfully he liveth.' For a certain great man, that had purchased much lands, a thousand marks by year, or I wot not what; a great portion he had: and so on the way, as he was in his journey towards London, or from London, he fell sick by the way; a disease took him, that he was constrained to lie upon it. And so being in his bed, the disease grew more and more upon him, that he was, by his friends that were about him, godly advised to look to himself, and to make him ready to God; for there was none other likelihood but that he must die without remedy. He cried out, 'What, shall I die?' quoth he. 'Wounds! sides! heart! Shall I die, and thus go from my goods? Go, fetch me some physician that may save my life. Wounds and sides! Shall I thus die?' There lay he still in his bed like a block, with nothing but, 'Wounds and sides, shall I die?' Within a very little while he died indeed; and then lay he like a block indeed. There were black gowns, torches, tapers, and ringing of bells; but what is become of him, God knoweth, and not I.

But hereby this ye may perceive, that it is not the abundance of riches that maketh a man to live quietly and blissfully. But the quiet life is in a mediocrity. *Mediocres optime vivunt*: 'They that are in a mean do live best.' And there is a proverb which I read many years ago, *Dimidium plus toto*; 'The half sometimes more than the whole.' The mean life is the best life and the most quiet life of all. If a man should fill himself up to the throat, he should not find ease in it, but displeasure; and with the one half he might satisfy his greedy appetite. So this great riches never maketh a man's life quiet, but rather troublous. I remember here a saying of Salomon, and his example: *Conservavi mihi argentum et aurum*, 'I gathered silver and gold together,' saith he; 'I provided me singers, and women which could play on instruments, to make men mirth and pastime: I get me psalteries and songs of music, &c., and thus my heart rejoiced in all that I did.' But what was the end of all this? *Cum convertissem me ad omnia*, &c., 'When I considered,' saith Salomon, 'all the works that my hands had wrought, &c., lo! all was but vanity and

vexation of mind; and nothing of any value under the sun.'
Therefore leave covetousness; for, believe me, if I had an enemy,
the first thing that I would wish to him should be, that he might
have abundance of riches; for so I am sure he should never be
in quiet. But think ye there be not many that would be so hurt?
But in this place of the gospel Christ spake and declared this
unquietness and uncertainty of great riches by a similitude and
parable of a great rich man, who had much land, that brought
forth all fruits plentifully; and he being in a pride of the matter,
and much unquiet by reason that he had so much, said to
himself, 'What shall I do, because I have not room enough
wherein to bestow my fruits, that have grown unto me of my
lands? I will thus do,' saith he; 'I will pull down my barns, and
build greater barns; and I will say to my soul, My soul, thou hast
much goods laid up in store for many years; take thine ease, eat,
drink, and be merry.' But God said to him, *Stulte, hac nocte
animam tuam repetunt abs te*: 'Thou fool! thou fool! this night will
they take thy soul from thee again, and then whose shall those
things be which thou hast provided? Even so it is with him,'
saith Christ, 'that gathereth riches unto himself, and is not rich
toward God,' &c. But yet the covetous man can never be
content. I walked one day with a gentleman in a park, and the
man regarded not my talk but cast his head and eye this and
that way, so that I perceived he gave no great ear to me; which
when I saw, I held my peace. At last, 'Oh,' quoth the gentleman,
'if this park were mine, I would never desire more while I lived.'
I answered and said, 'Sir, and what if ye had this park too?' For
there was another park even hard by. This gentleman laughed
at the matter. And truly I think he was diseased with the
dropsy: the more he had, the more covetous he was to have still
more and more. This was a farmer that had a farm hard by it;
and if he might have had this park to it, he would never have
desired more. This was a farmer, not altogether so covetous a
man as there be many now-a-days, as for one gentleman to rake
up all the farms in the country together into his hands all at
once.

And here one suit more to your highness: there lacketh one
thing in this realm, that it hath need of; for God's sake make

some promoters.[1] There lack promoters, such as were in king Henry the Seventh's days, your grandfather. There lack men to promote the king's officers when they do amiss, and to promote all offenders. I think there is great need of such men of godly discretion, wisdom, and conscience, to promote transgressors, as rent-raisers, oppressors of the poor, extortioners, bribers usurers. I hear there be usurers in England, that will take forty in the hundred;[2] but I hear of no promoters to put them up. We read not, this covetous farmer or landed man of the gospel bought corn in the markets to lay it up on store, and then sell it again. But, and if it please your highness, I hear say that in England we have landlords, nay, step-lords I might say, that are become graziers; and burgesses are become regraters:[3] and some farmers will regrate and buy up all the corn that cometh to the markets, and lay it up on store, and sell it again at a higher price, when they see their time. I heard a merchantman say, that he had travailed all the days of his life in the trade of merchandise, and had gotten three or four thousand pounds by buying and selling of grain here within this realm. Yea, and (as I hear say) aldermen now-a-days are become colliers: they be both woodmongers and makers of coals. I would wish he might eat nothing but coals for awhile, till he had amended it. There cannot a poor body buy a sack of coals, but it must come through their hands. But this rich man that the gospel speaketh of was a covetous man: God had given him plenty, but that made him not a good man: it is another thing that maketh a good man. God saith, *Si non audieris vocem meam*, 'If thou obey not my voice,' &c. And therefore worldly riches do not declare the favour or disfavour of God. The scripture saith, *Nemo scit an sit amore dignus an odio*. God hath ordained all things to be good; and the devil laboureth to turn all things to man's evil. God

---

1 A species of informers who prosecuted offenders against the laws, and received part of the fines that were levied.
2 By the statute 37 Hen. VIII. c. 9. no person was allowed to receive more than 'ten in the hundred' on pain of forfeiting treble the profits received, with imprisonment and a 'fine and ransom at the king's will and pleasure'.
3 Middlemen.

giveth men plenty of riches to exercise their faith and charity, to confirm them that be good, to draw them that be naught, and to bring them to repentance; and the devil worketh altogether to the contrary. And it is an old proverb, 'the more wicked the more fortunate'. But the unquietness of this covetous rich man declareth the unquietness of the mind, that riches bringeth with it. First, they are all in care how to get riches; and then are they in more care how to keep it still. Therefore the Apostle saith, *Qui volunt divescere incidunt in tentationes varias;* 'They that study to get great riches do fall into many divers temptations.' But the root of all evil is covetousness. 'What shall I do?' saith this rich man. He asked his own brainless head what he should do: he did not ask of the scripture; for if he had asked of the scripture, it would have told him; it would have said unto him, *Frange esurienti panem tuum,* &c.; 'Break thy bread unto the hungry.' All the affection of men now-a-days is in building gay and sumptuous houses; it is in setting up and pulling down, and never have they done building. But the end of all such great riches and covetousness is this: 'This night, thou fool, thy soul shall be taken from thee.' It is to be understood of all that rise up from little to much, as this rich man that the gospel spake of. I do not despise riches, but I wish that men should have riches as Abraham had, and as Joseph had. A man to have riches to help his neighbour, is godly riches. The worldly riches is to put all his trust and confidence in his worldly riches; that he may by them live here gallantly, pleasantly and voluptuously. Is this godly riches? No, no, this is not godly riches. It is a common saying now-a-days among many, 'Oh he is a rich man: he is well worth five hundred pounds.' He is well worth five hundred pounds, that hath given five hundred pounds to the poor; otherwise it is none of his. Yea, but who shall have this five hundred pounds? For whom hast thou gotten this five hundred pounds? What saith Salomon? Ecclesiastes v. *Est alia infirmitas pessima quam vidi sub sole, divitiæ conservatæ in malum domini sui*: 'Another evil (saith he) and another very naughty imperfection, riches hoarded up and kept together to the owner's own harm': for many times such riches do perish and consume away miserably. 'Such a one shall sometime have a son,' said he, 'that shall be a very beggar, and live all in extreme penury.' O goodly riches, that one man shall get it, and another come to devour it! Therefore, *Videte et cavete ab avaritia*; 'See and beware of covetousness.' Believe God's words, for they will not deceive you nor lie. 'heaven and earth shall perish, but *Verbum Domini manet in æternum*; the word of the Lord abideth, and endureth for ever.' O this leavened faith, this unseasoned faith! Beware of this unseasoned faith. A certain man asked me this question, 'Didst thou ever see a man live long that had great riches?' Therefore saith the wise man, 'If God send thee riches, use them.' If God send thee abundance, use it according to the rule of God's word; and study to be rich in our Saviour Jesus Christ: to whom, with the Father and the Holy Ghost, be all honour, glory, and praise, for ever and ever. *Amen.*

The First Sermon on the Lord's Prayer Preached Before Katherine, Duchess of Suffolk (1552)

Matthew vi.9.
Our Father, which art in heaven.

I have entered of late in the way of preaching, and spoken many things of prayer, and rather of prayer than of any other thing: for I think there is nothing more necessary to be spoken of, nor more abused than prayer was by the craft and subtilty of the devil; for many things were taken for prayer when they were nothing less. Therefore at this same time also I have thought it good to entreat of prayer, to the intent that it might be known how precious a thing right prayer is. I told you,

First, What prayer is.

Secondarily, To whom we ought to pray.

Thirdly, Where, and in what place we ought to pay, And,

Fourthly, I told you the diversity of prayer, namely, of the common prayer, and the private.

Now at this present time I intend as by the way of a lecture, at the request of my most gracious lady, to expound unto you, her household servants, and other that be willing to hear, the right understanding and meaning of this most perfect prayer which our Saviour himself taught us, at the request of his disciples, which prayer we call the *Paternoster*. This prayer of our Lord may be called a prayer above all prayers; the principal and most perfect prayer; which prayer ought to be regarded above all others, considering that our Saviour himself is the author of it; he was the maker of this prayer, being very God and very man. He taught us this prayer, which is a most perfect schoolmaster, and commanded us to say it: which prayer containeth great and wonderful things, if a learned man had the handling of it. But as for me, such things as I have conceived by the reading of learned men's books, so far forth as God will give me his grace and Spirit, I will shew unto you touching the very meaning of it, and what is to be understood by every word contained in this prayer; for there is no word idle or spoken in vain. For it must needs be perfect, good, and of great importance, being our Saviour's teaching, which is the wisdom of God itself. There be many other psalms and prayers in scripture very good and godly; and it is good to know them: but it is with this prayer, the Lord's Prayer, I say, like as with the law of love. All the laws of Moses, as concerning what is to be done to please God, how to walk before him uprightly and godly, all such laws are contained in this law of love, *Diliges Dominum Deum tuum ex toto corde tuo, et in tota anima tua, et in tota mente tua; et proximum sicut teipsum*: 'Thou shalt love the Lord thy God with all thy heart, with all thy soul, and with all thy mind; and thy neighbour as thyself.' Even so is it with this prayer. For like as the law of love is the sum and abridgment of the other laws, so this prayer is the sum and abridgment of all other prayers: all the other prayers are contained in this prayer; yea, whatsoever mankind hath need of to soul and body, that same is contained in this prayer.

This prayer hath two parts: it hath a preface, which some call a salutation or a loving entrance; secondarily, the prayer itself. The entrance is this: *Cum oratis, dicite, Pater noster, qui es in cælis*; 'When ye pray, say, Our Father, which art in heaven.' As who should say, 'You christian people, you that bear the name of Christians, must pray so.'

Before I go any further, I must put you in remembrance to consider how much we be bound to our Saviour Christ, that he would vouchsafe to teach us to pray, and in this prayer to signify unto us the good-will which our heavenly Father beareth towards us. Now to the matter.

'Our Father'. These words pertain not to the petitions: they be but an entering, a seeking favour at God's hand: yet if we well weigh and consider them, they admonish us of many things and strengthen our faith wondrous well. For this word, 'Father,' signifieth that we be Christ's brother, and that God is our Father. He is the eldest Son: he is the Son of God by nature, we be his sons by adoption through his goodness; therefore he biddeth us to call him our Father; which is to be had in fresh memory and great reputation. For here we are admonished how that we be reconciled unto God; we, which before-times were his enemies, are made now the children of God, and inheritors of everlasting life. This we be admonished by this word, 'Father'. So that it is a word of much importance and great reputation: for it confirmeth our faith, when we call him Father. Therefore our Saviour, when he teacheth us to call God 'Father', teacheth us to understand the fatherly affection which God beareth towards us; which thing maketh us bold and hearty to call upon him, knowing that he beareth a good-will towards us, and that he will surely hear our prayers. When we be in trouble, we doubt of a stranger, whether he will help us or not: but our Saviour commanding us to call God, 'Father', teacheth us to be assured of the love and good-will of God toward us. So by this word 'Father', we learn to stablish and to comfort our faith, knowing most assuredly that he will be good unto us. For Christ was a perfect schoolmaster: he lacked no wisdom: he knew his Father's will and pleasure; he teacheth us, yea, and most certainly assureth us, that God will be no cruel judge, but a loving Father. Here we see what commodities we have in this word, 'Father'.

Seeing now that we find such commodities by this one word, we ought to consider the whole prayer with great diligence and earnest mind. For there is no word nor letter contained in this prayer, but it is of great importance and weight; and therefore it is necessary for us to know and understand it thoroughly, and then to speak it considerately with great devotion: else it is to no purpose to speak the words without understanding; it is but lip-labour and vain babbling, and so unworthy to be called prayer; as it was in times past used in England. Therefore when you say this prayer, you must well consider what you say: for it is better once said deliberately with understanding, than a thousand times without understanding: which is in very deed but vain babbling, and so more a displeasure than pleasure unto God. For the matter lieth not in much saying, but in well saying. So, if it be said to the honour of God, then it hath his effect, and

117

we shall have our petitions. For God is true in his promises: and our Saviour, knowing him to be well affected towards us, commandeth us therefore to call him Father.

Here you must understand, that like as our Saviour was most earnest and fervent in teaching us how to pray, and call upon God for aid and help, and for things necessary both to our souls and bodies; so the devil, that old serpent, with no less diligence endeavoureth himself to let and stop our prayers, so that we shall not call upon God. And amongst other his lets, he hath one especially wherewith he thinketh to keep us from prayer, which is, the remembrance of our sins. When he perceiveth us to be disposed to pray, he cometh with his craft and subtile conveyances, saying, 'What, wilt thou pray unto God for aid and help? Knowest thou not that thou art a wicked sinner, and a transgressor of the law of God? Look rather to be damned, and judged for thy ill doings, than to receive any benefit at his hands. Wilt thou call him "Father", which is so holy a God, and thou art so wicked and miserable a sinner?' This the devil will say, and trouble our minds, to stop and let us from our prayer; and so to give us occasion not to pray unto God. In this temptation we must seek for some remedy and comfort: for the devil doth put us in remembrance of our sins to that end, to keep us from prayer and invocation of God. The remedy for this temptation is to call our Saviour to remembrance, who hath taught us to say this prayer. He knew his Father's pleasure; he knew what he did. When he commanded us to call God our Father, he knew we should find fatherly affections in God towards us. Call this, I say, to remembrance, and again remember that our Saviour hath cleansed through his passion all our sins, and taken away all our wickedness; so that as many as believe in him shall be the children of God. In such wise let us strive and fight against the temptations of the devil; which would not have us to call upon God, because we be sinners. Catch thou hold of our Saviour, believe in him, be assured in thy heart that he with his suffering took away all thy sins. Consider again, that our Saviour calleth us to prayer, and commandeth us to pray. Our sins let us, and withdraw us from prayer; but our Saviour maketh them nothing: when we believe in him, it is like as if we had not sins. For he changeth with us: he taketh our sins and wickedness from us, and giveth unto us his holiness, righteousness, justice, fulfiling of the law, and so, consequently, everlasting life: so that we be like as if we had done no sin at all; for his righteousness standeth us in so good stead, as though we of our own selves had fulfiled the law to the uttermost. Therefore our sins cannot let us, nor withdraw us from prayer: for they be gone; they are no sins; they cannot be hurtful unto us. Christ dying for us, as all the scripture, both of the new and old Testament, witnesseth, *Dolores nostros ipse portavit*, 'He hath taken away or sorrows.' Like as when I owe unto a man an hundred pound: the day is expired, he will have his money; I have it not, and for lack of it I am laid in prison. In such distress cometh a good friend, and saith, 'Sir, be of good cheer, I will pay thy debts'; and forthwith payeth the whole sum, and setteth me at liberty. Such a friend is our Saviour. He hath paid our debts, and set us at liberty; else we should have been damned world without end in everlasting prison and darkness. Therefore, though our sins condemn us, yet when we allege Christ and believe in him, our sins shall not hurt us. For St John saith, *Si quis peccaverit, advocatum habemus apud Patrem, Jesum Christum justum*, 'We have an advocate with God the Father, Jesus Christ the righteous.' Mark that he saith, *Advocatum, non advocatos*. He speaketh singularly, not plurally. We have one advocate, not many; neither saints, nor any body else, but only him, and none other, neither by the way of mediation, nor by the way of redemption. He only is sufficient, for he only is all the doer. Let him have all the whole praise! Let us not withdraw from him his majesty, and give it to creatures: for he only satisfieth for the sins of the whole world; so that all that believe in Christ be clean from all the filthiness of their sins. For St John Baptist saith, *Ecce Agnus Dei qui tollit peccata mundi*, 'Behold the Lamb of God which taketh away the sins of the world.' Doth the devil call thee from prayer? Christ calleth thee unto it again: for so it is written, *In hoc apparuit Filius Dei, ut destruat opera diaboli*; 'To that end the Son of God appeared, to destroy the works of the devil.'

But mark here: scripture speaketh not of impenitent sinners;

Christ suffered not for them: his death remedieth not their sins. For they be the bondmen of the devil, and his slaves; and therefore Christ's benefits pertain not unto them. It is a wonderful saying that St John hath, 'Behold the Lamb of God, that taketh away the sins of the world.' The devil saith unto me, 'Thou art a sinner.' 'No,' saith St John, 'the Lamb of God hath taken away thy sins.' Item, *Habentes igitur Pontificem magnum qui penetravit cœlos, Jesum Filium Dei, accedamus cum fiducia ad thronum gratiæ, ut consequamur misericordiam*; 'We therefore having a great high Priest, which hath passed through the heavens, even Jesus the Son of God, let us with boldness go unto the seat of his grace, that we may obtain mercy.' O, it is a comfortable thing that we have an access unto God! Isaiah saith, *In livore ejus sanati sumus*; 'The pain of our punishment was laid upon him, and with his stripes are we healed.' Further, in the new Testament we read, *Huic omnes prophetæ testimonium perhibent, remissionem peccatorum accipere per nomen ejus omnes qui credunt in eum*; 'Unto the same bear all prophets witness, that all they do receive forgiveness of sins by his name, which believe on him.'

Now you see how ye be remedied from your sins; you hear how you shall withstand the devil, when he will withdraw you from prayer. Let us therefore not give over prayer, but stick unto it. Let us rather believe Christ our Saviour than the devil, which was a liar from the beginning. You know now how you may prevent him, how you may put him off and avoid his temptations.

There is one other addition afore we come to the petitions, which doth much confirm our faith and increase the same: *Qui es in cœlis*, 'which art in heaven'. These words put a diversity between the heavenly Father and our temporal fathers. There be some temporal fathers which would fain help their children, but they cannot; they be not able to help them. Again, there be some fathers which are rich, and might help their children, but they be so unnatural, they will not help them. But our heavenly Father, in that we call him, 'Father', we learn that he will help, that he beareth a fatherly love towards us.

'In heaven'. Here we learn that he is able to help us, to give us all good things necessary to soul and body; and is mighty to defend us from all ill and peril. So it appeareth that he is a Father which will help; and that he being celestial, he is able to help us. Therefore we may have a boldness and confidence, that he may help us: and that he will help us, where and whensoever we call, he saith, *Cœlum et terram impleo*, 'I fill heaven and earth.' and again, *Cœlum mihi sedes est, et terra scabellum pedum meorum*; 'Heaven is my seat, and the earth is my footstool.' Where we see, that he is a mighty God; that he is in heaven and earth, with his power and might. In heaven he is apparently, where face to face he sheweth himself unto his angels and saints. In earth he is not so apparently, but darkly, and obscurely he exhibiteth himself unto us; for our corrupt and feeble flesh could not bear his majesty. Yet he filleth the earth; that is to say, he ruleth and governeth the same, ordering all things according unto his will and pleasure. Therefore we must learn to persuade ourselves, and undoubtedly believe, that he is able to help; and that he beareth a good and fatherly will towards us; that he will not forget us. Therefore the king and prophet David saith, *Dominus de cœlo prospexit*, 'The Lord hath seen down from heaven.' As far as the earth is from the heaven, yet God looketh down, he seeth all things, he is in every corner. He saith, The Lord hath looked down, not the saints. No, he saith not so; for the saints have not so sharp eyes to see down from heaven: they be purblind, and sand-blind, they cannot see so far; nor have not so long ears to hear. And therefore our petition and prayer should be unto him, which will hear and can hear. For it is the Lord that looketh down. He is here in earth, as I told you, very darkly; but he is in heaven most manifestly; where he sheweth himself unto his angels and saints face to face. We read in scripture, that Abel's blood did cry unto God. Where it appeareth that he can hear, yea, not only hear, but also see, and feel: for he seeth over all things, so that the least thought of our hearts is not hid from him. Therefore ponder and consider these words well, for they fortify our faith. We call him 'Father', to put ourselves in remembrance of his good-will towards us. 'Heavenly' we call him, signifying his might and power, that he may help and do all things according to his will and pleasure. So it appeareth most manifestly, that there lacketh neither good-will nor power in him. There was once a prophet, which, when he was ill entreated of king Joash, said, *Dominus videat et requirat;* 'The Lord look upon it, and requite it.' There be many men in England, and other where else, which care not for God, yea, they be clean without God; which say in their hearts, *Nubes latibulum ejus, nec nostra considerat, et circa cardines cœli ambulat:* 'Tush, the clouds cover him that he may not see, and he dwelleth above in heaven.' But, as I told you before, Abel's blood may certify of his present knowledge. Let us therefore take heed that we do nothing that might displease his majesty, neither openly nor secretly: for he is every where, and nothing can be hid from him. *Videt et requiret,* 'He seeth, and will punish it.'

Further, this word 'Father' is not only apt and convenient for us to strengthen our faith withal, as I told you; but also it moveth God the sooner to hear us, when we call him by that name, 'Father'. For he, perceiving our confidence in him, cannot choose but shew him like a Father. So that this word, 'Father', is most meet to move God to pity and to grant our requests. Certain it is, and proved by holy scripture, that God hath a fatherly and loving affection towards us, far passing the love of bodily parents to their children. Yea, as far as heaven and earth is asunder, so far his love towards mankind exceedeth the love of natural parents to their children: which love is set out by the mouth of his holy prophet Esay, where he saith, *Num oblivioni tradet mulier infantem suum, quo minus misereatur filii uteri sui? Et si obliviscatur illa, ego tamen tui non obliviscar:* 'Can a wife forget the child of her womb, and the son whom she hath borne? And though she do forget him, yet will I not forget thee.' Here are shewed the affections and unspeakable love which God beareth towards us. He saith, *Nunquid potest mulier,* 'May a woman?' he speaketh of the woman, meaning the man too; but because women most commonly are more affected towards their children than men be, therefore he nameth the woman. And it is a very unnatural woman, that hateth her child, nor neglecteth the same. But, O Lord, what crafts and conveyances useth the devil abroad, that he can bring his matters so to pass, that some women set aside not only all motherly affections, but also all

122

natural humanity, insomuch that they kill their own children, their own blood and flesh! I was a late credibly informed of a priest, which had taken in hand to be a midwife. O what an abominable thing is this! But what followed? He ordered the matter so, that the poor innocent was lost in the mean season. Such things the devil can bring to pass; but what then? God saith, 'Though a woman do forget her children, though they kill them, yet will I not forget thee, saith the Lord God Almighty.' Truth it is, there be some women very unnatural and unkind, which shall receive their punishments of God for it; but for all that, we ought to beware and not to believe every tale told unto us, and so rashly judge. I know what I mean. There hath been a late such tales spread abroad, and most untruly. Such false tale-tellers shall have a grievous punishment of the Lord, when he shall come to reward every one according unto his deserts.

Here I have occasion to tell you a story which happened at Cambridge. Master Bilney, or rather Saint Bilney, that suffered death for God's word sake; the same Bilney was the instrument whereby God called me to knowledge; for I may thank him, next to God, for that knowledge that I have in the word of God. For I was as obstinate a papist as any was in England, insomuch that when I should be made bachelor of divinity, my whole oration went against Philip Melancthon and against his opinions. Bilney heard me at that time, and perceived that I was zealous without knowledge: and he came to me afterward in my study, and desired me, for God's sake, to hear his confession. I did so, and, to say the truth, by his confession I learned more than before in many years. So from that time forward I began to smell the word of God, and forsook the school-doctors and such fooleries. Now, after I had been acquainted with him, I went with him to visit the prisoners in the tower at Cambridge; for he was ever visiting prisoners and sick folk. So we went together, and exhorted them as well as we were able to do; moving them to patience, and to acknowledge their faults. Among other prisoners, there was a woman which was accused that she had killed her own child, which act she plainly and stedfastly denied, and could not be brought to confess the act; which denying gave us occasion to search for

the matter, and so we did. And at the length we found that her
husband loved her not; and therefore he sought means to make
her out of the way. The matter was thus: a child of hers had been
sick by the space of a year, and so decayed as it were in
consumption. At the length it died in harvest-time. She went to
her neighbours and other friends to desire their help, to prepare
the child to the burial; but there was nobody at home: every man
was in the field. The woman, in an heaviness and trouble of
spirit, went, and being herself alone, prepared the child to the
burial. Her husband coming home, not having great love
towards her, accused her of the murder; and so she was taken
and brought to Cambridge. But as far forth as I could learn
through earnest inquisition, I thought in my conscience the
woman was not guilty, all the circumstances well considered.
Immediately after this I was called to preach before his majesty,
and it was done at Windsor; where his majesty, after the sermon
was done, did most familiarly talk with me in a gallery. Now,
when I saw my time, I kneeled down before his majesty,
opening the whole matter; and afterwards most humbly
desired his majesty to pardon that woman. For I thought in my
conscience she was not guilty; else I would not for all the world
sue for a murderer. The king most graciously heard my humble
request, insomuch that I had a pardon ready for her at my return
homeward. In the mean season that same woman was delivered
of a child in the tower at Cambridge, whose godfather I was,
and Mistress Cheke was godmother. But all that time I hid my
pardon, and told her nothing of it, only exhorting her to confess
the truth. At length the time came when she looked to suffer: I
came, as I was wont to do, to instruct her; she made great moan
to me, and most earnestly required me that I would find means
that she might be purified before her suffering; for she thought
she should have been damned, if she should suffer without
purification. Where Master Bilney and I told her, that that law
was made unto the Jews, and not unto us; and that women lying
in child-bed be not unclean before God; neither is purification
used to that end, that it should cleanse from sin; but rather a
civil and politic law, made for natural honesty sake; signifying,
that a woman before the time of her purification, that is to say,

as long as she is a green woman, is not meet to do such acts as other women, nor to have company with her husband: for it is against natural honesty, and against the commonwealth. To that end purification is kept and used, not to make a superstition or holiness of it, as some do; which think that they may not fetch neither fire nor any thing in that house where there is a green woman; which opinion is erroneous and wicked. For women, as I said afore, be as well in the favour of God before they be purified as after. So we travailed with this woman till we brought her to a good trade; and at the length shewed her the king's pardon, and let her go.

This tale I told you by this occasion, that though some women be very unnatural, and forget their children, yet when we hear any body so report, we should not be too hasty in believing the tale, but rather suspend our judgments till we know the truth. And again, we shall mark hereby the great love and loving-kindness of God our loving Father, who sheweth himself so loving unto us, that notwithstanding women forget sometimes their own natural children, yet he will not forget us; he will hear us when we call upon him; as he saith by the evangelist Matthew: 'Ask, and it shall be opened unto you', &c. Then he cometh and bringeth in a pretty similitude, saying: "Is there any man amongst you, which, if his son asked bread, will offer him a stone? If ye then', *cum sitis mali*, 'being evil, can give your children good gifts', &c. In these words, where he saith, *cum sitis mali*, 'which be evil', he giveth us our own proper name; he painteth us out, he pincheth us; he cutteth off our combs; he plucketh down our stomachs. And here we learn to acknowledge ourselves to be wicked, and to know him to be the well-spring and fountain of all goodness, and that all good things come of him. Therefore let every man think lowly of himself, humble himself and call upon God, which is ready to give us not only bread and drink, or other necessaries, but the Holy Ghost. To whom will he give the Holy Ghost? To lords and ladies, to gentlemen or gentlewomen? No, not so. He is not ruled by affections: he hath not respect unto personages. *Poscentibus*, saith he, 'unto those which call upon him', being rich or poor, lords or knights, beggars or rich; he is ready to give unto them when they come to him. And this is a great comfort unto those which be poor and miserable in this world; for they may be assured of the help of God, yea, and as boldly go unto him, and desire his help, as the greatest king in earth. But we must ask, we must inquire for it; he would have us to be importunate, to be earnest and diligent in desiring; then we shall receive when we come with a good faith and confidence. To whom shall we call? Not unto the saints. *Poscentibus illum*, saith he. Those that call upon him shall be heard. Therefore we ought to come to him only, and not unto his saints.

But one word is left, which we must needs consider; *Noster*, 'our'. He saith not 'my', but 'our'. Wherefore saith he 'our'? This word 'our' teacheth us to consider that the Father of heaven is a common Father; as well my neighbour's Father as mine; as well the poor man's Father as the rich: so that he is not a peculiar Father, but a Father to the whole church and congregation, to all the faithful. Be they never so poor, so vile, so foul and despised, yet he is their Father as well as mine: and therefore I should not despise them, but consider that God is their Father as well as mine. Here may we perceive what communion is between us; so that when I pray, I pray not for myself alone, but for all the rest: again, when they pray, they pray not for themselves only, but for me: for Christ hath so framed this prayer, that I must needs include my neighbour in it. Therefore all those which pray this prayer, they pray as well for me as for themselves; which is a great comfort to every faithful heart, when he considereth that all the church prayeth for him. For amongst such a great number there be some which be good, and whose prayer God will hear: as it appeared by Abraham's prayer, which prayer was so effectuous, that God would have pardoned Sodome and Gomorre, if he might have found but ten good persons therein. Likewise St Paul in shipwreck preserved his company by prayer. So that it is a great comfort unto us to know that all good and faithful persons pray for us.

There be some learned men[1] which gather out of scripture,

---

1 St Augustine observes: 'Si martyr Stephanus non sic orasset, ecclesia Paulum hodie non haberet.' Sermon 382.

that the prayer of St Stephen was the occasion of the conversion of St Paul. St Chrysostom saith, that that prayer that I make for myself is the best, and is of more efficacy than that which is made in common.[1] Which saying I like not very well. For our Saviour was better learned than St Chrysostom. He taught us to pray in common for all; therefore we ought to follow him, and to be glad to pray one for another: for we have a common saying among us, 'Whosoever loveth me, loveth my hound.' So, whosoever loveth God, will love his neighbour, which is made after the image of God.

And here is to be noted, that prayer hath one property before all other good works: for with my alms I help but one or two at once, but with my faithful prayer I help all. I desire God to comfort all men living, but specially *domesticos fidei*, 'those which be of the household of faith'. Yet we ought to pray with all our hearts for the other, which believe not, that God will turn their hearts and renew them with his Spirit; yea, our prayers reach so far, that our very capital enemy ought not to be omitted. Here you see what an excellent thing prayer is, when it proceedeth from a faithful heart; it doth far pass all the good works that men can do.

Now to make an end: we are monished here of charity, and taught that God is not only a private Father, but a common Father unto the whole world, unto all faithful; be they never so poor and miserable in this world, yet he is their Father. Where we may learn humility and lowliness: specially great and rich men shall learn here not to be lofty or to despise the poor. For when ye despise the poor miserable man, whom despise ye? ye despise him which calleth God his Father as well as you; and peradventure more acceptable and more regarded in his sight than you be. Those proud persons may learn here to leave their stubbornness and loftiness. But there be a great many which little regard this: they think themselves better than other men be, and so despise and contemn the poor; insomuch that they will not hear poor men's causes, nor defend them from wrong and oppression of the rich and mighty. Such proud men despise

1   St Chrysostom frequently teaches the very opposite.

the Lord's prayer: they should be as careful for their brethren as for themselves. And such humility, such love and carefulness towards our neighbours, we learn by this word 'Our'. Therefore I desire you on God's behalf, let us cast away all disdainfulness, all proudness, yea, and all bibble-babble. Let us pray this prayer with understanding and great deliberation; not following the trade of monkery, which was without all devotion and understanding. There be but few which can say from the bottom of their hearts, 'Our Father'; a little number. Neither the Turks, neither the Jews, nor yet the impenitent sinners, can call God their Father. Therefore it is but vain babbling, whatsoever they pray: God heareth them not, he will not receive their prayers. The promise of hearing is made unto them only which be faithful and believe in God; which endeavour themselves to live according unto his commandments. For scripture saith, *Oculi Domini super justos*; 'The eyes of the Lord are over the righteous, and his ears open unto their prayers.' But who are those righteous? Every penitent sinner, that is sorry from the bottom of his heart for his wickedness, and believeth that God will forgive him his sins for his Son our Saviour Jesus Christ's sake. This is called in scripture 'a just man', that endeavoureth himself to leave all wickedness. In such sort Peter and Paul were just, because they did repent, and believe in Christ, and so endeavoured themselves to live according unto God's laws. Therefore like as they were made just before God, so may we too; for we have even the self-same promise. Let us therefore follow their ensample. Let us forsake all sins and wickedness; then God will hear our prayers. For scripture saith, *Dominus facit quicquid volunt timentes eum, et clamorem eorum exaudit ac servat eos*: 'The Lord fulfileth the desire of them that fear him; he also will hear their cry, and help them.' In another place he saith, *Si manseritis in sermone meo, et verba mea custodiveritis, quicquid volueritis petentes accipietis*: 'If ye abide in me, and my words abide in you, ask what ye will, and it shall be done for you.' So we see that the promises pertain only to the faithful; to those which endeavour themselves to live according to God's will and pleasure; which can be content to leave their wickedness, and follow godliness: those God will hear at all times, whensoever they shall call upon him.

Remember now what I have said: remember what is meant by this word 'our'; namely, that it admonisheth us of love and charity; it teacheth us to beware of stubbornness and proudness; considering that God loveth as well the beggar as the rich man, for he regardeth no persons. Again, what is to be understood by this word 'Father'; namely, that he beareth a good will towards us, that he is ready and willing to help us. 'Heavenly', that admonisheth us of his potency and ability, that he is ruler over all things. This, I say, remember, and follow it: then we shall receive all things necessary for this life; and finally everlasting joy and felicity. *Amen.* Let us pray, 'Our Father'.